J. D. Greear has the rare ability to take p
simple and readable. His writing is so str
you might not even realize how much you're learning as you read. I can
confidently say that whether you are a new Christian or a seasoned
disciple, you will not look at God the same after reading this book.

CLAYTON KING, teaching pastor, NewSpring Church,
author of *Stronger* and *Overcome*

When J. D. Greear's gift of plain-spokenness meets with the doctrine
of God, the church is sure to be better for it. He offers a much-needed
remedy for those prone to worship at the altar of introspection: God is
bigger than you imagine, the most worthy and practical object of your
contemplation, and the wellspring of your unshakeable joy.

JEN WILKIN, author and Bible teacher

In *Not God Enough*, J. D. Greear takes on what are perhaps the most
weighty and important questions of our day. His insights and answers
are both transformational and transferable. This is more than a book.
Not God Enough is a resource you will use for years to come.

ANDY STANLEY, senior pastor,
North Point Ministries

Too many Christians today are following a tepid, docile, half-baked
version of God, who fits comfortably in their preconceived notions
and Sunday morning schedules. My friend J. D. Greear has written a
new book, *Not God Enough*, that is must-read for every Christian. It's
a call to worship the true God of the Bible—bigger, deeper, and more
unpredictable than we can know. I highly recommend it.

GREG LAURIE, senior pastor,
Harvest Ministries

In *Not God Enough*, J. D. Greear has given us an invaluable resource
showing us how most of our spiritual dysfunctions go back to a view
of God that is too small. If you want a faith that burns with white-hot

intensity and that can endure the seasons of trial or temptation, this book will take you there.

DANIEL L. AKIN, president,
Southeastern Baptist Theological Seminary

My friend J. D. Greear understands both the gospel and the struggles of ordinary people. In *Not God Enough*, he shows us that no matter what our spiritual problem, there is one solution—a great, big God.

BRYAN LORITTS, lead pastor,
Abundant Life Christian Fellowship,
author of *Saving the Saved*

With extraordinary transparency, wit, and wisdom, J. D. shows us how the ordinary problems we face—fear, insecurity, apathy, and doubt—go back to a faulty view of ourselves and our God. By helping us regain a larger view of God, he will show you the way to escape make-believe Christianity and grow into a more authentic and vibrant faith. You'll love this book—you'll not only be encouraged, but you'll also be deeply challenged!

ELYSE M. FITZPATRICK, author of
Finding the Love of Jesus from Genesis to Revelation

J. D. is my pastor. One thing is clear; he understands the power of God over the earth, even over troubling events of today. J. D. has helped shape my view of God in spite of the racial tension and divided Christian voice on current social issues. He has displayed boldness on issues that are routinely ignored by the church, due in part to his faith in the ultimate control of God. He believes great things about God and then leads us to attempt great things for God. This book will shape you to do the same.

TERRANCE RUTH, PhD, executive director
of the North Carolina NAACP State Conference

NOT

GOD

ENOUGH

NOT GOD ENOUGH

WHY YOUR SMALL GOD LEADS TO BIG PROBLEMS

J. D. GREEAR

ZONDERVAN®

ZONDERVAN

Not God Enough
Copyright © 2018 by J. D. Greear

Requests for information should be addressed to:
Zondervan, *3900 Sparks Dr. SE, Grand Rapids, Michigan 49546*

ISBN 978-0-310-33786-7 (ebook)

Names: Greear, J. D., 1973- author.
Title: Not God enough : why your small God leads to big problems / J.D. Greear.
Description: Grand Rapids, Michigan : Zondervan, [2017]
Identifiers: LCCN 2017031818 | ISBN 9780310337775 (softcover)
Subjects: LCSH: God (Christianity) | God (Christianity)—Knowableness.
Classification: LCC BT103 .G735 2017 | DDC 231—dc23 LC record available at https://
    lccn.loc.gov/2017031818

Art direction: Faceout Studio / Tim Green
Interior design: Denise Froehlich

First printing December 2017 / Printed in the United States of America

23 24 25 26 27 LBC 9 8 7 6 5

You shall love the Lord your God with all your heart and with all your soul and with all your mind.

MATTHEW 22:37 (ESV)

To my mother and father, Lynn and Carol Greear,
and my mother-in-law and father-in-law, Ann and
Ron McPeters, who taught Veronica and me from our
earliest years the reality of God's presence, lived it out
before us, and never gave us any reason to doubt it.

CONTENTS

FOREWORD

The brilliant Robert Dick Wilson was professor of Old Testament at Princeton Theological Seminary from 1900 to 1929. One of his students during that time was the famous preacher-to-be, Donald Grey Barnhouse.

Twelve years after he graduated from Princeton, Barnhouse was invited back to preach in chapel. As Barnhouse stood up to preach, he noticed his old teacher sitting down near the front of the pulpit. When chapel ended, Dr. Wilson approached his student, extended his hand, and said, "If you come back again, I will not hear you preach. I only come once. I am glad that you are a big Godder. When my boys come back, I come to see if they are big Godders or little Godders, and then I know how their ministry will be."

Not sure he understood his teacher's words, Barnhouse asked him to explain.

"Well," said Dr. Wilson, "Some men have a little God, and they are always in trouble with him. He can't do any miracles. He doesn't intervene on behalf of his people. They have a little God, and I call them little Godders. Then there are those who have a great God. He speaks and it is done. He commands and it stands fast. He knows how to show himself strong on behalf of those who fear him."

Then Dr. Wilson paused for a moment, smiled, and said to Barnhouse, "You have a great God, and he will bless your ministry. God bless you."

I read this story many years ago when I was just getting started as a preacher, and since then I have had a growing aspiration to be a big Godder, to truly believe in the miracle-working power and greatness of God. I cannot give you an objective report on my progress, but I would like to tell you what I know about the author of the book you are about to read.

Without reservation, I can say that J. D. Greear is a big Godder. In 2001, he became the lead pastor of what today is The Summit Church in Raleigh-Durham, North Carolina. Three hundred people were attending the church when he took over, and last year The Summit Church was the thirty-sixth largest church in America with an attendance north of ten thousand. It is also, according to *Outreach Magazine*, one of the fastest growing churches in America, adding over six hundred new congregants in the last year alone. Because J. D. Greear believes great things about God, he has attempted great things for God.

In this book, he teaches us that our view of God ultimately shapes what happens in our lives. In the words of A. W. Tozer, "The most portentous fact about any man is . . . what he in his deep heart conceives God to be like. We tend by a secret law . . . to move toward our mental image of God." In other words, when we imagine a little God, we assume he can only do little things.

With inspiring quotes and riveting stories, J. D. makes the biblical truths about God come alive. Beginning with the story of Moses and his encounter with God at the burning bush, we are introduced to the power, love, wisdom, and majesty of God in such a powerful way that we will want to pause periodically and worship. J. D. believes that when we see God as Moses saw him, our hearts will glow like Moses's face did. And radical life change will be the result.

One of the great takeaways from this book is its apologetic content. In his response to those who want to make God responsible for all the tragedies in the world, J. D. writes, "In many cases, we have to live out our days not knowing the precise reason for terrible events.

But the cross shows us what they *cannot* mean. They cannot mean that God is absent or out of control."

Often when you hear someone say, "My God would never do that" or similar statements, they are not talking about the God of the Bible, in whose image they were created. Rather, they are talking about a god they have created for themselves. In the chapter titled "You Don't Get Your Own Personal Jesus," J. D. reminds us that God said, "I am who I am," not "I am whoever you want me to be."

The discussion of God's wrath and his love fill the pages of the final chapters. I don't think I turned a page without stopping to write something down that I wanted to remember. I shared some of J. D.'s insights about the crucifixion, which are found in the eleventh chapter, when I officiated at a recent communion service.

Not God Enough concludes with a call to action. In J. D.'s words, "Christianity . . . makes a terrible hobby," and "You cannot place the sun of God's glory into orbit in your life." The God of the Bible demands our highest allegiance, our total adoration, and our unconditional obedience.

Twenty years ago, I went through two bouts of cancer. I ultimately had a stem cell transplant which cured me of the disease. When I came back to my pulpit after several weeks of recovery, I stood in front of the church I have now pastored for thirty-six years, and my message was simply, "God Is Enough." This is the glorious message of this book that I have been blessed to read and honored to endorse.

DAVID JEREMIAH

ACKNOWLEDGMENTS

In *Freedom of Conscience*, Martin Luther warned prospective pastors against aspirations of teaching the worldwide church. Instead, he said, focus on your church. If the worldwide church feels like you have something helpful to say to it, Luther advised, it will come to you. To that end, every book I have written has been written first and foremost for The Summit Church in Durham, North Carolina, which I have been privileged to pastor for sixteen years. I love its members, and our staff team is the greatest group of people ever assembled on earth. The Summit congregation are such a grateful and generous people. They have patiently listened as I worked through the questions this book addresses, and many more, weekend by weekend. They truly yearn to see God in all his glory.

I also want to thank the excellent editorial team at Zondervan, including Sandy Vander Zicht, Amanda Sorenson, John Sloan, and Matt Estel, for believing in this message and working so tirelessly to craft it into a form I could share.

Sealy Yates and his team at Yates and Yates believed in this message before anybody else and fought fiercely to preserve its integrity. Sealy Yates is truly an agent without equal.

My preaching and writing would not be half of what it is without the expert help of Dr. Chris Pappalardo, and his input shows up in countless ways throughout this book. Chris's one-line job description is "Make me sound smarter." A frustrating assignment, no doubt, but rest assured that the things that do sound smart in this book originated with him. Thanks also to a new team member, Allison Dolbeer, who fact-checks, source-checks, occasionally just shakes her head and says, "No way," and keeps us from embarrassing ourselves. Or at least she tries.

There is no more capable, dedicated, and selfless administrative team than what God has provided for me in Dana Roland Leach and Aly Rand. Dr. David Thompson, our lead executive pastor, is a friend and colaborer whose dedication to our church and my ministry enables me to devote my time to teaching. I am grateful for his friendship and his selflessness. Curtis Andrusko and Chuck Reed have spoken endless words of courage and vision into me throughout this project, specifically about the subjects contained herein. They shield and inspire me.

My wife, Veronica, never ceases to amaze me in how selflessly she guards my time so that I can spend time writing and studying. She is my greatest earthly gift. And our four kids, Kharis, Allie, Ryah, and Adon, are the joy of my life. May the faith of their fathers become theirs as well.

PART 1

GOD IS

A god small enough to be understood is not big enough to be worshipped.

EVELYN UNDERHILL

I CAN'T BELIEVE!

For much of my life, I have struggled with faith. I always *wanted* to believe, knew that I was supposed to believe, and hoped deep down inside that I really did believe. But more often than I cared or dared to admit, the pillars of my faith felt shaky. I didn't have the bold, daring, passionate faith that I knew I should have, and I longed for it. For a pastor, that's not good for business.

But I struggled to comprehend why a loving God would leave the world in the shape it's in. And I wasn't satisfied with the standard answer—that suffering makes us stronger and that bad things always lead to good things. There didn't seem to be any "silver lining" that would justify something as horrific as the Holocaust.

Or why would a good, loving God create a hell? I understand that there's got to be some punishment for wickedness—but *hell*? I get angry at my enemies and want payback, but I wouldn't want to do *that* to them. So why does God? Why not make them do hard labor for a few thousand years, change their hearts so they feel sorry for what they did, and then move on?

And if God wants so desperately for the world to be saved, why isn't *he* doing more about it? He is God after all, and he writes the rules. So why not appear to every world leader like he did Saul, the first-century persecutor of Christians, and turn them into an "apostle Paul" devoted to spreading the message (Acts 9:1–4)? If God really loves lost sons and daughters as passionately as he implies in the story of the prodigal son, *why leave their rescue in the hands of people like us*? Surely, if *God* were serious about the mission, he could find a more efficient means of saving the world he loves than through the efforts of this feeble, inconsistent body of people we call the church. Why not send a band of angels to get the job done? He's God. Who's stopping him?

Furthermore, why wasn't God answering my questions? Surely, he could see I *wanted* to believe in him. Why make belief so hard? Why be silent when I really needed him to speak?

Maybe you haven't asked these exact questions, but my guess is that you've probably asked some of your own. Almost no thinking person I know hasn't looked at the world at some point and thought, "God, why aren't you doing more?"

This past summer, when my family and I worked with a group of Syrian refugees, my eight-year-old daughter asked, "Dad, if God loves these people so much, why doesn't he fix all this?"

I told her, "He is, sweetheart. He's using us to do it." A standard pastor answer.

Not satisfied, she pressed back, "But why doesn't he do something about it *himself*?"

It's a fair question. Why not send that army of angels we've heard so much about and make the war in Syria go away? Why do Syrian children have to pay the price for the greedy injustice of others?

These "whys" and many others stood in the way of a confident, passionate faith in God.

A FAITH THAT FELL SHORT

Nearly twenty-five years ago, I chose to believe in Jesus because I could find no other satisfactory explanation for his life, death, and resurrection other than that he really is who he said he was. His life, his teaching, his fulfillment of prophecy, his beautiful character, and his resurrection from the dead all overwhelmingly demonstrated that Jesus really was divine. No one else in history has ever been like him. It seemed obvious to me that he couldn't have been a liar, a lunatic, or a legend that grew over time. He is the Son of God.

Even after being convinced of that, however, my questions about his ways kept me from a confident faith.

I struggled to really *love* him. The "Great Commandment" says to *love* God with all your heart, soul, and mind (Matt 22:37), and I wanted to obey it. I wanted to be deeply and passionately in love with God. I wanted to pant for him like a parched deer pants for a bubbling brook, like King David described (Ps 42:1). Brother Lawrence, the seventeenth-century dishwashing monk, talked about the "inexpressible sweetness" he tasted in God's presence. He said his emotions about God were "so charming and delicious that I am ashamed to mention them."[1] To be honest, I'm not even sure what he's talking about. But whatever he had, I wanted it.

Some people in my church seemed to love God like that. One woman in our church tears up every single time she starts talking about God's grace. She seems sincere. I wondered why no tears ever came to my eyes when I did. I knew how to play the game, of course. I knew when to raise my hands and close my eyes and how to nod my head slowly and grunt when other Christians said something profound. I had perfected that pensive, inquisitive, squinted-eyes face that communicates "I'm spiritual too" in a religious conversation. Yet often the actual emotions weren't there. And that disturbed me.

I'm not saying that I felt *no* love or desire for God or that deep down I didn't really believe. I did. But my bewilderment about God's ways felt like an obstacle keeping my heart from releasing itself fully to him. I wanted to find the certainty of faith and the passion, confidence, and joy that goes with it. But I didn't have it, and I didn't even know where to look for it.

When I was seventeen years old, I walked forward at a campfire commitment service one Sunday night in front of five hundred other high school and college students and threw my stick into the fire, symbolically declaring that I was ready to offer my whole life as a living sacrifice to Jesus. I sang, "The world behind me, the cross before me," as loudly as anyone that night.

I followed up my commitment with action. After graduating from college, I lived as a missionary in Southeast Asia. Life was hard there—the culture, food, and life-rhythms were very different from what I had grown up with in the American South. I had never been to Asia before and didn't speak the language. When the plane landed, the only things I could say in their language were "Hi, my name is J. D.," "Where is your bathroom?" and "My house is on fire." But I gave myself fully to the task. I learned the language and adapted to the culture. Yet even jumping in headfirst as a missionary didn't resolve the lack of passion I felt in my relationship with God. I heard stories of missionaries who cheerfully gave up their lives in service to Jesus, but I didn't feel like suffering for his name would be "pure joy."

My second year there, a visiting mission team I brought in was caught distributing Bibles and imprisoned. An angry mob burned their cars and demanded that the police release them so that they could kill them. I lived less than fifteen minutes away from where all this was going down, and a friend came to me and told me that the mob's leaders were looking for me too because they assumed I was connected. I was escorted home and ordered by local police not to leave my house because I was under investigation.

Sitting alone that night, I knew I was supposed to be thinking about what a joy it was to go through all this, what an honor it was to suffer for the name of Christ. But that's not what I was thinking about. I was thinking about how scared I was and how much I wanted to go home. It's one thing to stand by a campfire and say that you're ready to die for Jesus, and it's quite another when you think someone is about to take you up on the offer.

Why didn't I feel the passionate love for Jesus that others did? I *wanted* to be ready to die for him, but I wasn't. Sacrifice felt like a burden. Worship felt like an obligation. And why did I struggle so much *just to believe*? Did I have any business on the front lines when I was still so shaky on the basics?

THE BEGINNING OF BOLD FAITH

I've come to see that the problem—my lack of faith, my passionless heart, and my struggle to surrender—came from a fundamental deficiency in my vision of God. The God I imagined in my heart was not the same God who reveals himself through the Scriptures. I had traded the true God for a much smaller version.

I hadn't done this intentionally. I didn't have an idol shrine set up in my basement, nor was I cutting out sections of the New Testament like Thomas Jefferson famously did. I acknowledged the truthfulness of every sentence of Scripture. But in my heart I assumed the God behind it all was only a slightly bigger, slightly smarter, slightly better version of me. I thought he would act in ways I could comprehend and easily follow. When I couldn't, it made me wonder if he existed at all.

I am, in part, the product of a Christian culture that has fostered and promoted a small, domesticated view of God. The Western Christianity in which I have been immersed focuses on the practicality of faith. We present God as the best way to a happy and prosperous life. We show how God is the best explanation for unanswered questions and the best means to the life we desire. Our worship services seem more like pep rallies accompanied by practical tips for living than encounters with the living God who stands beyond time and whose presence is indescribably glorious. These shallow glimpses of God are fine as long as our faith remains untested, but they are utterly insufficient in the midst of serious questioning or intense suffering.

Ironically, our "diminished" God feels, for a while, *easier* to believe in. He acts in ways we can understand, explain, predict, and even control. He rarely offends us, so we are not embarrassed to talk about him with our friends. He helps us find our meaning and purpose. We think everyone should give him a try.

But in the end such a God cannot sustain faith. He cannot account for the complexities of creation or the mysteries of suffering. He'll never incite passion, devotion, or *worship*. He's too small. "A god small enough to be understood," the British philosopher Evelyn Underhill observed, will never be "big enough to be worshipped."[2]

Furthermore, my small view of God kept me from grasping how wicked my sin against him actually was and what an act of mercy it was for him to save me. I confessed, of course, that I was a sinner in need of grace, but I didn't sense, deep in my heart, my desperate need for mercy. I raged against the concept of hell because I didn't think *I* really deserved it—and if I didn't really deserve it, why did anyone else? So, like the Pharisees who scoffed at the forgiven prostitute weeping with love at Jesus's feet, I didn't love God that much because—like them—deep down I didn't think I had been forgiven of that much (Luke 7:47).

Finally, because I thought of God as only a slightly bigger, slightly smarter version of me, I couldn't accept that he might do things in ways I wouldn't expect. Thus, I had a hard time believing that the love demonstrated at the cross was reflective of who he really was. If he really was loving, I surmised, there wouldn't be Syrian refugees. His love at the cross didn't move me because his magnificence in the heavens hadn't humbled me.

The book of Proverbs says that the fear of God is the "beginning of knowledge" (Prov 1:7). That means that without a trembling awe before God's majesty, we'll never develop the ability to *know* him, much less love him. In other words, if we want to think properly *about* God, we must first stand properly humbled *before* him. The posture of humility is a *prerequisite* for faith. Until we have a sense of his magnitude, we won't even be able to ask the right questions of him, much less receive his answers.

True worship is intimacy grounded in awe. Awe, which Solomon says must come first, stands silent before the *awesomeness* of God's majesty. Only then can worship move to intimacy, which grows out of embracing how close this infinite God has brought himself to us in the cross. Only the two *together*, in the right order, lead to biblical faith. Only the two together will yield the emotion that fulfills the Great Commandment and fuel the passion that pursues the Great Commission.

As Tim Keller says, "If our prayer life discerns God only as lofty, it will be cold and fearful; if it discerns God only as a spirit of love, it will be sentimental."[3] However, when we behold God as he really is— the Creator greater than the cosmos and the Savior of the cross—we become trusting, passionate, confident, zealous worshipers.

SO YOU DOUBT? JOIN THE CLUB

Sometimes people in my church ask me sheepishly, "Pastor, have you ever had doubts?" I always say "no" just to mess with them.

Every year I teach a class for college students at our church on the "hard" questions of the Christian faith. I started one class by saying, "If you've ever doubted the truth of Scripture, that demonstrates the depravity of your heart and proves that you're not really a Christian." I let it hang there for a minute as a general sense of panic settled in. Then I said, "Of course that's not true. Every thinking Christian I know doubts."

In fact, many of the *greatest* Bible heroes doubted—and some quite dramatically. Moses doubted God *after* God appeared to him at the burning bush. Think about that. A piece of shrubbery was *talking* to him, and Moses talked back *disrespectfully*. David filled his psalms with outbursts of frustration and confusion toward God, psalms that never seem to make it into the lyrics of popular

Christian radio songs. Imagine singing this one next Sunday to the tune of "Friend of God":

> Why, LORD, do you reject me
> and hide your face from me? . . .
> You have taken from me friend and neighbor—
> darkness is my closest friend. (Ps 88:14, 18)

Job asked so many doubt-laden questions that God finally had to say, "Enough! Stop talking," like he was quieting a toddler. But then he made Job write down all his questions so later generations could recognize their questions in his. John the Baptist, Jesus's cousin, doubted whether Jesus really was the Messiah (Luke 7:18–19)—this *after* seeing the Spirit of God descend upon him like a dove and hearing the voice of God from heaven declare, "This is my beloved Son" (Matt 3:17 ESV). After seeing a manifestation of the third person of the Trinity while standing in front of the second and hearing the voice of the first, you can doubt? Maybe there is hope for me.

My favorite account of doubt in the Bible is Matthew's description of the disciples as they watched Jesus ascend back to heaven:

> "And when they saw him they worshiped him, but some doubted" (Matt 28:17 ESV).

Think about this: *Jesus is floating in the air*, and some are still saying, "I don't know. I'm still undecided."

You ask, "But how could they doubt *then*, after they'd seen the miracles, heard the voice from heaven, and watched him fly away like Superman?" It's because some of the things Jesus did—or didn't do—were baffling to them (Luke 24:21; Acts 1:6). If he really was the Messiah, why wasn't he overthrowing the Romans? Surely the Messiah would at least do that. Why was he leaving when there were still sick people? And had he really just given them the task of testifying about him to every nation and then left without so much as providing them with a travel budget?

They had thrown their stick into the fire. They had walked the aisle. They were all in. But Jesus's behavior was making it hard to keep believing.

I have good news for those of you who struggle with doubt: doubt in the Christian life is not only normal; it is divinely orchestrated. At least the questions that *lead* to doubt are. Charles Spurgeon, the famed British preacher of the nineteenth century, once told his congregation that doubt was like a foot poised in the air, prepared to step either forward or backward. Yes, doubt can drive you backward into unbelief, but you can never go forward in faith until you raise your foot. God therefore puts us in situations that make us ask the questions to get us to raise our foot. Sometimes it's the only way we will ever take a step forward in our knowledge of him.

Doubt happens when the superficialities of your faith meet the realities of this world. Many of us *inherited* our faith—from our parents, friends, or even the surrounding culture. But God doesn't want secondhand faith. Each of us has to learn to trust God on our own. At some point, *you* must choose to step out of the boat like Peter, trusting Jesus to hold you up. You can't ride piggyback on someone else's shoulders.

Doubt, as I hope to show you in this book, reveals those places you have shrunk God down to your size. Doubts can help you see where you have put expectations on God that arise out of what you *think* he should do rather than what he has *said* he will do.

I'll be so bold as to say that if you've never doubted, you're probably not that deep in your faith. So, in that sense, I hope I can help you learn to doubt a little—to boldly raise your foot so God can draw you forward, deeper into him. Doubt can lead you to awe, and awe can lead you to worship.

WHAT WE THINK ABOUT GOD IS THE MOST IMPORTANT THING ABOUT US

In this book, I want to give you a vision, as best I can, of God as he really is. Not the domesticated, practical, fix-it-and-make-you-feel-good god of Western Christianity, but the real God. This book is about how you can know and trust and love this God. It's about how to hear God when he speaks. It's about understanding what humility before him looks like. It's about discovering that he really is for you and that his Spirit lives in you. It's about knowing that God is big enough, that he cares enough, and that you can trust him.

Decades ago, American pastor A. W. Tozer wrote about the importance of our personal "vision" of God:

> What comes into our minds when we think about God is the most important thing about us. . . . No religion has ever been greater than its idea of God. . . . We tend by a secret law of the soul to move toward our mental image of God.

Tozer added,

> The most [determining] fact about any man is not what he at a given time may say or do, but what he in his deep heart conceives God to be like.[4]

What we think about God determines *everything* else in our lives: what we value, what we pursue, and how we pursue it. Our vision of God also determines whether our beliefs will make it through the inevitable storms of doubt, temptation, and suffering that life brings. The real God is not a god who simply completes us and makes us feel sentimental during worship; he is a God who humbles us and transforms us from the inside out. When you really see him, you'll either love him or hate him. The one thing you will not be is bored.

BURNING BUSHES AND GLOWING FACES

In order to discover this awesome God, we are going to delve into the faith encounters of several biblical heroes, but there's one in particular we will keep coming back to: *Moses*.

More people cite Moses as the architect of their faith than any other person in history. It may surprise you, then, to know that Moses's personal faith journey was quite rocky. He had numerous doubts, missteps, and failures in faith. I believe God fashioned Moses's story that way because he wanted Moses's experience to be both a comfort to us when we doubt and an example of how to follow God in the midst of doubt.

Of course, the details of our stories will not parallel Moses's exactly. You probably shouldn't expect any of your shrubbery to burst into flames, and it's unlikely you'll lead your disgruntled coworkers out of a stifling work environment by miraculously making a way through the outdoor fountains. But the core of Moses's experience—how God got Moses's attention, what God said to him, and how Moses responded—are all examples of how we can trust and follow God.

Perhaps the most significant moment in Moses's faith journey was the afternoon he came face to face with God's glory—or, at least, face to "back parts." On that day, God put Moses in the cleft of a rock, covered him with his hand, and then passed right in front of him. As God passed by, he removed his hand so Moses could see the "back parts" of glory (Exod 33:23 KJV). Moses's face glowed so radiantly afterward that he had to veil his face to keep it from burning people's eyes.

The apostle Paul points to that encounter as the pattern for *all* spiritual growth in our lives: "And we all, who with unveiled faces [in contrast to Moses] contemplate the Lord's glory, are being transformed into his image with ever-increasing glory" (2 Cor 3:18). When we see God like Moses saw him, our hearts will glow like Moses's face did. We will catch fire with trust, passion, and love. Spiritual life does not come from discipline or mastery of doctrine. It comes from divine *vision*.

And here's the amazing thing: we get to see something even greater than Moses did! Moses only got to see the back parts of God's glory, but in the life of Jesus we behold God's very *face*. The apostle John writes that in Jesus "we have seen [God's] glory, the glory of the one and only Son, who came from the Father, full of grace and truth. . . . No one has ever seen God, but the one and only Son, who is himself God and is in closest relationship with the Father, has made him known" (John 1:14, 18). In Jesus, we see a God of infinite holiness who was willing to become sin for us so sinners could see him without dying. We see a God of infinite majesty willing to humble himself to die a traitor's death to save those who betrayed him. The strength of a flame, Saint Athanasius said, is demonstrated not by its ability to burn upward but by its ability to burn *down*. In Jesus we get to see God's glory as he humbles himself to die for rebellious sinners.

When God opens our eyes to see the beauty of Jesus, his glory bursts through the cloud of our questions. When we truly behold his glory, we won't need to be *compelled* to trust or love God; we just will. In the depth of our hearts, we will be *convinced* that he's a God worth living and dying for. Others will see in our demeanor a confidence that goes far beyond personality, charisma, or dogma. They will sense in our hearts a burning passion fueled by a genuine encounter with a glorious and living God.

If that's the kind of encounter you want to have, keep reading.

CHAPTER 2

YOUR GOD IS TOO SMALL

When I was a kid, my greatest ambition was to meet Michael Jordan. I was a nine-year-old North Carolinian when he hit the game-winning shot against Georgetown to secure the second national championship for the University of North Carolina. From that point on, "Air Jordan" became more than just my favorite basketball player: he was my role model. I wanted to be like Mike.

I was convinced that if I worked hard enough I could play just like him. So, my friends and I lowered our basketball goals to seven feet and spent endless hours perfecting our split-legged, tongue-extended dunks. Those dunks felt so "right" when I was doing them, but when I watched the videos later, they just didn't quite look like his. And when I watch those videos now, all I can think is, "Lord Jesus, what was wrong with me?" I look more like a wounded duck coming in for a crash landing than an athlete soaring over the competition.

You can imagine how excited I was when, during my eighth-grade year, I found out that Air Jordan was going to participate in a charity golf tournament not far from my house. I couldn't care less about golf, and I had no clue what charity we were support-ing, but my best friend and I set out early that morning for the tournament with only one agenda: to meet the man, the myth, the legend himself. For eight hours, we followed his caravan around the course.

We never even got close. His bouncers clearly had experience with people like us.

That is, until the very end of the day. I was standing, discouraged, near the golf course exit waiting for my parents to pick me up. That's when I saw it: a purple Porsche Carrera 944, winding its way down the road toward the exit. I knew it immediately: *Michael.*

With all the discretion and poise you would expect from a thirteen-year-old, I turned around and yelled to my friend, "It's HIM! It's Jordan!" A couple dozen people heard me and ran over to where I was standing. As Jordan approached, he slowed down his car and rolled down his window, apparently looking for someone. My best friend saw his opportunity. Before I knew what was happening, he grabbed my shoulders and shoved me in through Jordan's passenger window.

There I was, less than three inches from the face of the man I had idolized for the past five years. I was so close I could have licked him (and one of my lifelong regrets is that I did not). I nervously sputtered out, "Hi, Mike." The six-foot-six megastar cut a sideways glance at me and said, "Dude, get out of my car." I pulled my head out, turned to the crowd, put my hands up in the air, and yelled, "He talked to me! He talked to me!"

Being in the presence of greatness has a strange effect on us. We feel a curious mixture of desire and terror. We're not sure whether we want to draw close or run away.

If being in the presence of *human* greatness makes us feel that way, what is it like to be in the presence of *infinite* greatness? If I was that starstruck in the presence of someone whose glory consisted of the fact that he could jump thirty-six inches higher than me, what is it like to find yourself in the presence of the One who spoke the universe into existence?

BIGGER THAN BIG

Ironically, many today seem turned off by the concept of an awesome, terrifyingly great God. We assume that a God you need to fear must be guilty of some kind of fault, or that a terrified reaction to an infinitely great and wise God is a relic leftover from an oppressive, archaic view of religion. We prefer a God who is small and domesticated, who thinks like we think, likes what we like, and whom we can manage, predict, and control.

We only have to glance upwards at the night sky to see how ridiculous that is.

A couple summers ago, my family and I spent some time out in the African bush. We were amazed by how many more stars we could see there than we could from our home in Raleigh, North Carolina. Miles away from the nearest electric light, with no light pollution to obstruct our vision, it felt like we were seeing *millions* of stars. Astronomers tell us, however, that it's only 9,096. That's how many stars are visible to the naked eye—about 1/100,000,000,000,000,000,000 of what's actually out there. They estimate the number of stars right now to be about three septillion, and that number is constantly expanding. That's a three with twenty-four zeros after it, or a number that looks like this:

$$3,000,000,000,000,000,000,000,000$$

If you're like me, numbers like million, billion, trillion, or a septillion tend to sound all the same after a while. Most of us are satisfied if we open our bank account and see a number with two digits. The magnitude of a number followed by twenty-four zeros exceeds our comprehension. It's what I experience when I hear someone talk about the national debt, or when I look at the amount my mortgage statement says I will actually pay on my house over thirty years.

See if this helps: one *million* seconds ago takes you back about eleven days. Can you remember what you were doing eleven days ago?

What about a *billion* seconds ago? Do you remember what you were doing a billion seconds ago?

That's thirty-one years and eight months ago.[1] Sometime in the 1980s. The compact disc player had just been released. Rambo was saving our world from certain destruction. The Jedi were returning for the first time. Some of you, of course, can't remember what you were doing then because there was no "you" to speak of.

How about a *trillion* seconds ago? How long ago do you think that would be? A couple centuries back? Maybe a few millennia?

A trillion seconds ago was 29,672 BC.

A million seconds ago: 11 days.

A billion: 32 years.

A trillion: 32,000 years.

And those are *seconds*. Little things, so small that they fly by without us knowing. Now think about the fact that there are at least three *septillion* stars, each one putting out roughly the same amount of energy as a *trillion* atom bombs *every second*. Some are so big they defy description—like Eta Carinae in our own Milky Way, which is five million times brighter than our sun!

These stars exist in an expanse we simply cannot comprehend. The Hubble Telescope is now sending back faint, infrared images of galaxies we didn't even know about, estimated at twelve billion light years away. And there are likely more beyond that.

All of them were created in a single moment with a single word from God.

Not only that, the prophet Isaiah tells us that God calls each of these three septillion stars *by name* (Isa 40:26). That idea alone overwhelms me. We can't even come up with distinctive names for the 9,096 stars we see in the night sky! We've given a few of them cool "star-sounding" names like Beta Draconis or Betelgeuse, but the vast majority have names like SAO-067173. Yet God has a special name for each of those three septillion. What does he call them? Bob? Apollinarius? T-3.14159-er? And every cubic inch of those stars is composed of billions of trillions of atoms. If each of those atoms have names, God knows them too. He knows what is going on with every subatomic particle of every atom at every moment.

I can't remember all the names of the people in my small group. Or what I did last Friday. Honestly, I just thought about it for five minutes, and I still can't remember what I did last Friday. Can you?

The God who created such an incomprehensively immense universe and intimately knows every millimeter of it can't just be thought of as big. He's bigger than big. He's bigger than all the words we use to say "big." He is not just "huge," "gigantic," "humongous," or "gargantuan." We have no words or measurements to express his magnitude or power.

And see, here's the thing: the universe, as expansive as it is, still has its limits. It is finite. God is *eternal*. He exists outside the farthest expanses of our universe, holding it all, as Isaiah says, in the palm of his hand. He palms the universe like Jordan palms a basketball.

The reality of God's immensity *must* shape the way we approach him and how we respond to him when he speaks to us.

Moses thought he knew who God was. As a kid, he'd heard the stories about the God who chose his ancestor Abraham and promised to make his family into a great nation. But when Moses encountered that God at the burning bush, he experienced a God far beyond anything he had imagined.

COME . . . BUT NOT TOO CLOSE

While Moses was tending sheep in the desert one afternoon, he saw a strange sight: a bush that burned without burning up. Curious, he walked toward it. He had no idea he was about to encounter the Creator of the galaxies that he gazed up at every night from the mountain.

As Moses drew close,

God called to him from within the bush, "Moses! Moses!"

> And Moses said, "Here I am."
>
> "Do not come any closer," God said. "Take off your san-
> dals, for the place where you are standing is holy ground." ...
> At this, Moses hid his face, because he was afraid to look at
> God. (Exod 3:4–6)

God proceeded to tell Moses that he had chosen him to lead his
people (the children of Israel) to a place where they could live as his
treasured possession. Moses responded by saying,

> Suppose ... they ask me, "What is his name?" Then what
> shall I tell them? God said to Moses, "I AM WHO I AM. This
> is what you are to say to the Israelites: 'I AM' has sent me
> to you.' ...
>
> This is my name forever;
>   the name you shall call me
>   from generation to generation." (Exod 3:13–15)

By asking God for his name, Moses was not simply trying to figure out what to call God. In those days, names conveyed important
information about you: where you came from, whom you belonged
to, or your status. Moses was asking God for his credentials: "What
are you in charge of?"

God didn't respond with a name Moses expected, and certainly
not with the list of credentials Moses was asking for. He simply
replied with "I AM." "I am" is a verb phrase, of course, not a name.
By answering this way God is saying, "Moses, you can't relate to me
like anything or anyone else. I am beyond categories, descriptions,
and words. You can't grasp where I came from or how I came to be.
I just am. Are you willing to accept that?"

The burning bush itself served as a metaphor for God's name.
Just like Moses could not understand how the bush burned with-
out burning up, he also could not comprehend the magnitude of the
God speaking *through* this bush. Moses could not deny the presence

of the mysterious bush or the sound of the voice speaking through it. The question was: Was this really *God*?

Obviously, if Moses were hearing the voice of the I AM, this was no time for matching wits. He wasn't in the position to have a "meeting of the minds." If this is the God who fashioned the heavens and exists outside of time, he's not the kind of God you pull up next to and have a chat with. You certainly don't stick your head inside his car and think about licking his face. Moses's questions would have to wait.

The overwhelming greatness of God demanded one response from Moses: humble surrender. Only from that posture would Moses be able to receive what God said next. So Moses took off his sandals—a sign of respect in the presence of greatness. And then he listened.

This wasn't the only time Moses encountered God, and the second encounter was much like the first. In Exodus 34, God appeared to Moses again, and in this second encounter God explained to Moses why in all their communication Moses had never seen God's face. If he did, God explained, Moses would die: "And the LORD said, 'I will cause all my *goodness* to pass in front of you. . . . But,' he said, 'you cannot see my face, for no one may see me and live'" (Exod 33:19–20, emphasis mine).

Think about it: *What kind of being is so magnificent, holy, and good that merely seeing his face would kill you?* Notice what's so dangerous for Moses. It isn't God's anger or even his wrath. Nor is it some physiological component of God that would blind him—some kind of effervescent, radioactive energy that would melt Moses's face off. It was God's *goodness* that would kill him. We don't usually think of goodness as dangerous or frightening. What kind of goodness is so good that merely seeing it kills you?

Have you ever been around someone whose kindness and love was so great that it made you feel ashamed of yourself? I felt that way when I met the famous missionary Elisabeth Elliot. She faithfully served the Lord for several years among the Huaorani people in Ecuador, even after her husband had been murdered by those same tribespeople. When I met her, she was in her eighties. Her life was a nearly untarnished record of selfless, humble faithfulness. She seemed so heroic, so selfless that I didn't even know what to say. Standing before her, I just felt ashamed. All I could think about was how selfish and petty I was.

Multiply that emotion of inadequacy by a septillion and maybe you'll feel something resembling the shame sinful people feel in the presence of God. To be in his presence is to come face to face with a greatness so immense that the human mind implodes trying to think about it and a goodness so good that sin simply dies in its presence.

THE BEGINNING OF WISDOM

Faith begins in awestruck fear. As we saw in the previous chapter, King Solomon taught that any knowledge of God begins with fear (Prov 1:7). Fear even precedes our ability to hear.

"The fear of God" was the step I tried to skip in my faith. That's partially because I am an American, and I don't like the idea of something beyond my comprehension, something I can't control, something I can't reduce down to a *Believing for Dummies* book. (I literally own a book titled *God for Dummies*.) We want a God who will restore us to peaceful equilibrium, take away our stress, and promise us a blissful afterlife. Most Christians haven't rejected God; they have just reduced him.

As the prophet Isaiah said, the first evidence of God working in your life is not a warm and fuzzy feeling of peace but a fear that makes us *tremble*: "This is the one to whom I will look: he who is humble and contrite in spirit and trembles at my word" (Isa 66:2 ESV).

When you ask your questions of God, do you *tremble*? Do you approach him with a sense of how large, glorious, and wise he must be if he spoke the world into existence?

Even if you are not sure you believe in God, do you approach the concept of him sensing that *if he is there* he is not just a bigger, slightly wiser version of you? Surely you should expect that if he really does exist, much of what he says will go against your preconceived notions.

Do you approach the great and magnificent Creator with your proverbial sandals off?

If not, you won't know what to do with his voice when you hear it.

NOT JUST AN OLD TESTAMENT THING

Maybe you're thinking Moses's experience is some kind of Old Testament thing, and now that Jesus has come we've moved on to the "New and Improved" Testament, where God gets a PR makeover. God-the-cranky-detention-hall-teacher gets replaced by Jesus-the-meek-and-mild, who likes to toss children into the air and snuggle with lambs.

Yes, the tenderness of Jesus is amazing, but I've got news for you: *every single person who got a glimpse of Jesus's glory in the New Testament responded in exactly the same way Moses did.* When Peter first recognized Jesus for who he was, he fell on his face and begged to get away (Luke 5:8). When Peter experienced Jesus's glory again on the Mount of Transfiguration, he "fell facedown to the ground, terrified" (Matt 17:6).

My favorite is Mark's recording of what the disciples did when they saw Jesus calm a storm on the Sea of Galilee. They'd set off late one afternoon to get to the other side of the sea. As they sailed, "A great windstorm arose, and the waves were breaking into the boat, so that the boat was already filling. But [Jesus] was in the stern, asleep on the cushion. And they woke him and said to him, 'Teacher, do you not care that we are perishing?'" (Mark 4:37–38 ESV).

Now this must have been *some* storm. These were experienced fishermen who had been in lots of storms, and this one was so bad that they cried out in terror, sure they were going to die.

Finally, Jesus stood up in the boat, calmly wiped the sleep out of his eyes, and "rebuked the wind and said to the sea, 'Peace! Be still!'" (Mark 4:39 ESV).

You rebuke something you have authority over, like a parent with a child. Jesus stands up and rebukes the weather like it's nothing more than an unruly adolescent. No incantations, no loud invectives or chants, no magic wands or *expecto patronums*. In Greek he literally says, "Be quiet and *stay* quiet!" In other words, he put the storm in time out. The storm slunk away like a scolded puppy.

At that point, Mark says that the disciples, who had been afraid in the storm, went from afraid to *greatly* afraid (Mark 4:40–41). When they were in the storm, certain they were going to die, they were afraid—just plain old, regular, "think-we're-going-to-die" afraid. But after Jesus rescued them, they were *terrified*.

In other words, *the rescue scared them more than the storm*. Seeing Jesus's power *over* the storm was more terrifying than thinking they were going to die *in* the storm.

The apostle John had a similar encounter when he saw Jesus for the first time after his ascension. Keep in mind, John had been one of Jesus's closest earthly friends (John 13:23). They were buds. John had rather confidently described himself as "the disciple whom Jesus loved," which I've always thought took a lot of nerve to put in print. (Imagine changing your email signature to "Sam, the brother my dad really likes.") John felt so close with Jesus that he reclined his head on Jesus's chest during the last supper (John 13:23). I've got some close guy friends, but I don't have many (read: any) close enough that they rest their head on my chest during dinner. John and Jesus were close.

What does this reunion between these two BFFs involve? A high-five? A warm embrace or a big hug? Let John describe it in his own words:

I turned around to see the voice that was speaking to me. And when I turned I saw seven golden lampstands, and among the lampstands was someone like a son of man, dressed in a robe reaching down to his feet and with a golden sash around his chest. The hair on his head was white like wool, as white as snow, and his eyes were like blazing fire. His feet were like bronze glowing in a furnace, and his voice was like the sound of rushing waters. In his right hand he held seven stars, and coming out of his mouth was a sharp, double-edged sword. His face was like the sun shining in all its brilliance. When I saw him, I fell at his feet as though dead. (Rev 1:12–17)

When John saw Jesus in glory, John didn't burst into a peppy chorus of "Friend of God." He fell at Jesus's feet *as though he were dead*. That's not a figure of speech. He literally thought he was going to die.

Jesus gave John this vision, however, because John and his church were about to go through an intense time of persecution. Jesus knew the only thing that would sustain them during a time like that was a vision of himself sitting victoriously above it all. If they were going to endure the terrors of the tribulation, they needed to see someone more awesome than the tribulations were terrible. They didn't need a Jesus who was merely the missing piece in their dissatisfied lives. They needed a Jesus who ruled the universe. Only a glorious and mighty Savior would give them confidence to face the horrors of the apocalypse.

Maybe the reason we have trouble boldly persevering in faith through pain and trial is because we've never seen Jesus this way. You see, when life caves in on you—whether that's caused by the horsemen of the apocalypse or an unexpected cancer diagnosis— you need more than a sentimental Jesus sitting beside you stroking your hand, explaining that there's a silver lining or spewing non-sensical platitudes about things that don't kill you only making you stronger. You need a God of infinite glory who sits upon the throne of the universe, who has promised to marshal every molecule in the universe in pursuit of his plan and your good, who stands behind your salvation and will let nothing stand in his way (Eph 1:3–14).

Maybe the reason we don't long for Jesus's return the way John did (Rev 22:20) is that we've never *seen* him the way John did. Maybe that's also the reason we don't overcome the Enemy the way his generation did (Rev 12:11).

DOESN'T PERFECT LOVE CAST OUT FEAR?

Now, you may be asking, "Wait. Fear God? But the Bible says that God is love! Doesn't the Bible describe him as the Shepherd tenderly holding the lost sheep and the broken-hearted Father running to welcome home his lost son?"

Yes. But forgiveness like that should lead us to *more* fear, not less. The cross, which Jesus had to endure to obtain our forgiveness, first illustrates for us how terrifying it is to offend God's justice. The cross, Paul says, demonstrated God's *righteousness* (Rom 3:25), that is, his rightful anger toward sin. There, we see the awful price our rebellion against God deserved. Beholding God from the safety of the cross is like watching a tornado pass in front of you from the safety of a cave. You may be safe, but you still tremble before the awesome power of the tornado, a power that could sweep you away if you stepped out of that cave for even a second.

In the Psalms, King David explains,

> But with you there is forgiveness,
> *that you may be feared.* (Ps 130:4 ESV, emphasis mine)

Think about the irony of that statement. The experience of forgiveness leads to *fear*? Yes. From the safety of forgiveness, we can better understand the glory of the God who provided it. As John Newton, repentant slave-trader and writer of "Amazing Grace," explained,

'Twas grace that taught my heart *to fear*,
and [then] grace my fears relieved.

Those who understand their forgiveness tremble *more*, not less, in God's presence. They stand amazed at the magnitude of the God who holds them safely in his arms. So when they think about God, or pray, or ask questions of him, they do so with a sense of hushed awe. They recognize the size of the God they are speaking to.

YOU CAN'T SKIP 101

Just like I did, many of us try to skip this step—the fear of God—in our pursuit of faith. But we can't. The fear of God precedes faith. It fuels our adoration of him and undergirds our understanding of his love. Worship, faith, passion, and obedience can flourish only in the soil of awestruck wonder. No fear, no faith.

Many of us have never grasped that God is a being of unfathomable magnitude, wisdom, and goodness. We have not rejected God; we have reduced him. We assume we are on the same playing field with him. Because we have never considered how much greater his wisdom must be than ours, how much higher his ways, or how much purer his thoughts, we think a few more answers— just a little more explanation—would satisfy us.

We're wrong. We don't need more information. We need to behold the living God, whose greatness is so great that it makes our minds explode when we try to comprehend him and whose goodness is so good we can't tell if we want to draw closer or run away.

Our diminished view of God has also severely hampered our witness to a skeptical world. The sentimental Precious Moments God, who offers pat answers and rides around in the passenger seat of our lives making things smoother and happier, fails to offer a sufficient explanation for the glories, tragedies, and mysteries of the universe. Albert Einstein's student Charles Misner reportedly explained that this was the reason Einstein was never interested in church:

> The design of the universe is very magnificent. . . . In fact, I believe that is why Einstein had so little use for organized religions, although he struck me as basically a very religious man. Einstein must have looked at what the preachers said about God and felt that they were blaspheming! He had seen more majesty than he had ever imagined in the creation of the universe and felt the God they were talking about couldn't have been the real thing. My guess is that he simply felt that the churches he had run across did not have proper respect for the Author of the Universe.[2]

So which do you want—a god you can understand or a God you must fear?

A God we can predict, instruct, and control is not a God who will captivate our affections or command our devotion. *He's not God enough.* He's a God we can never really trust because he is not wise or glorious enough to account for the glories and tragedies of our existence. *Because we have made him small enough to be understood, he is no longer big enough to be worshiped.*

Simple logic will show us, however, that only a God of inestimable size could have created the universe. Only a God of perfect righteousness can fulfill our longings for justice. And, as we will see, only a God of unfathomable grace would be willing to redeem us.

This is the kind of God whose greatness we crave, whose presence makes us want to both draw close and run away. This is the kind of God we find speaking to us in the Bible.

CHAPTER 3

HE IS NOT SILENT

When I heard the voice come out of that little speaker, it felt like an angel was calling my name from heaven. Prior to that moment, I'd never even noticed the little speaker located on the control panel in the elevator. But for the greater part of an hour it had become the most important thing in my life. I glanced at it every ten seconds.

Earlier that afternoon, I'd squeezed onto that elevator with fourteen of my pastor friends. (I know it sounds like the beginning of a joke, but it's true.) Our destination was the sixth floor of the United States Capitol offices where we had an appointment to visit with the chief representative for Muslim relations in the United States government. We were running a few minutes behind, and so to save time all fifteen of us mashed ourselves into one little elevator car.

No problem. It would be a short ride. And surely if there's one place in the world you can count on everything working properly, it's Washington, DC.

The elevator had another idea. Between the third and fourth floors it came to a complete and sudden halt like a Republican Congress with a Democratic president. And there we hung, suspended between the third and fourth floors for over an hour. In August. With no air conditioning. Fifteen pastors wearing suits and ties. Sweating. Thirsty. And nothing makes you have to use the bathroom like knowing you can't physically get to one!

We pressed the emergency call button repeatedly, but nothing happened.

That's when I noticed another elevator feature I had never noticed before: the "maximum weight capacity" warning. Apparently, you were not supposed to load more than eight moderately sized fifth-grade girls on that elevator. According to a quick mental calculation, we had exceeded that limit by the weight of a minivan.

The Muslim imam we were going to meet—who had a great sense of humor—came to the other side of the fourth-floor door and started hollering, "Pray to Jesus! Maybe he will resurrect the elevator!"

Eventually we pried the elevator door open and got someone on the fourth-floor landing to do the same, creating a small, two-foot gap barely big enough to squeeze one of us through. Just as we were about to hoist the first one of us up and out, the speaker crackled to life. The voice on the other end of the line said, "I am with the elevator company. Please hang tight and don't move. Someone will be there within five minutes to get you out."

We told her we already had the situation well in hand and explained our ingenious exit strategy. "No!" she said. "*Please* do not do that. If the elevator drops even a few feet while you are crawling out, it could cut you in half. Hang on and we will help you."

So we paused from our potentially "divisive" pursuit and waited. Eventually the fire department got us out. We each had sweat off about six pounds, but none of us had been cut in half. A win-win situation.

Somehow, we manage to go through life like I did on that elevator—oblivious to the fact there is a "speaker" right in front of us. That speaker bears the quiet voice of God, but we typically bound through life ignoring it. But then something happens—sometimes something traumatic—that turns our attention to it. In the chaos of life, we hear a voice whispering, or maybe shouting, at us. It may not answer all our questions, but it tells us that we are not alone and that help is coming for us. The voice lets us know, in the words of Francis Schaeffer, that God is there, and he is not silent.[1]

Whether or not you choose to listen to that voice is the most important decision of your life.

A VOICE FROM A BURNING BUSH

We don't know much about Moses's faith during the years he grew up in Pharaoh's house or during the forty years he wandered in the wilderness after his first disastrous attempt to deliver Israel. We don't know if Moses was even interested in God on the day that God spoke to him. We do know that Moses was a discouraged and defeated fugitive, probably in his sixties, leading a flock of his father-in-law's sheep in the desert—which sounds to me like the ultimate life-fail. Most likely, his primary concern that day, as it was every day, was finding grass and water for his flock. But when he saw a flaming bush that wasn't being reduced to ashes, he turned aside to see what was going on: *"When the Lord saw that he turned aside to see,* God called to him from out of the bush, 'Moses! Moses!' And he said, 'Here I am.'"* (Exod 3:4 ESV, emphasis mine).

Notice that when Moses turned aside, the voice did not explain *how* the fire was burning in the bush. Nor did God explain where he had been for four hundred years, a question Moses and every living Israelite wanted the answer to. The voice simply called out to Moses, "I am here, and I have something to say to you."

After four hundred years, with no explanation, the silence was broken. The God who spoke the heavens into existence began to converse with Moses: "I've been watching you, Moses. I haven't forgotten you, and I've seen your anguish and heard your cries" (Exod 3:7, my paraphrase).

Moses didn't encounter God because he finally figured God out or because he finally looked behind the rock where God had been hiding. Moses encountered God because God came to where Moses was and called his name.

THE VOICE STILL SPEAKS TODAY

In the same way, most people who find God don't do so because they discern his existence as the logical conclusion of a disciplined philosophical enquiry. Most find God in a moment where they were confronted with the simple fact that *God is*. They are going through life unsuspectingly when suddenly—**boom**—God interrupts.

For many outside the church, God often does this like he did Moses, through unresolved mysteries—burning bushes. He confronts us with things we can't explain, things that invite us to look beyond the day-to-day tasks.

For some of us, it is the simple question of where we all came from. In his late seventies, Antony Flew, one of the twentieth century's most famous philosophers, stunned the philosophical world by announcing that he had begun to believe in God. If you are not into philosophy, you may not realize what a big deal this was. It would be like Rush Limbaugh suddenly declaring that he is a Democrat. Flew said he just didn't see any other compelling explanation for the complexities of design in creation. For years he had tried to make peace with it, but it just couldn't be that nothing times nobody equaled everything. It couldn't be that the wonderful, beautiful complexity and intelligence of life emerged from a dead chaos. There had to be, as scientist Thomas Edison had previously concluded, "a captain on the bridge."

For others, the bleakness of death prompts them to consider the possibility of something beyond the grave. Shortly before he died, Steve Jobs, the founding CEO of Apple, told an interviewer that he sometimes believed in God and sometimes didn't. But after he was diagnosed with cancer, he found himself *wanting* to believe. It can't be that when we die it all just fades to black. All the wisdom we've accumulated as a human race, all our accomplishments, somehow must live on. In fact, he explained, that's why he never liked to put on/off switches on Apple devices. He didn't like the idea of being able just to flip a switch and turn something off.[2]

In the same way, the experience of love and beauty are invitations to turn aside and listen. C. S. Lewis said that through beauty he experienced a yearning that compelled him to earnestly search for its source, as if he were feeling a ray of sunshine warm his face, knowing there must be some sun from which it emanates. He concluded,

> A baby feels hunger: well, there is such a thing as food. A duckling wants to swim: well, there is such a thing as water. Men feel sexual desire: well, there is such a thing as sex. If I find in myself a desire which no experience in this world can satisfy, the most probable explanation is that I was made for another world. If none of my earthly pleasures satisfy it, ... well, earthly pleasures were never meant to satisfy it, but only to arouse it, to suggest the real thing.[3]

I find that much more compelling than the ways people like atheist Richard Dawkins account for beauty: when you look at a certain scenery, you think it's beautiful because your ancestors believed that there was food out there, and that particular neurological feature helped them survive and has now come down to you.[4]

Really? Do you find the stars and sunsets beautiful because subconsciously they remind you of Twinkies? Is your love toward your spouse, kids, or parents merely a conditioned response that enables you to propagate your DNA into society faster than your neighbors? Try putting that on a Valentine's Day card: "On this very special day, my genes are releasing chemical compounds into my bloodstream because they have been cultivated through centuries of evolution to see you as particularly useful for the propagation of my DNA into the next generation." If you truly believe that, I'm impressed with your intellectual consistency. But I'd advise you to downplay that perspective on Valentine's Day.

Perhaps pain or disappointment has driven you to look upward for answers. A professional athlete once confided to me that tragedy in his life was forcing him to consider things he'd never considered before. He graduated college as an all-American, was drafted in the first round by one of the premier teams in the nation, and awarded a contract for millions of dollars. One afternoon, he joined up with some buddies for some careless fun and ended up on his back with multiple broken bones. The circumstances of his accident nullified his contract. In the space of a few seconds, everything he'd lived for was gone. With tears in his eyes, he said, "I can't believe I threw it all away for a few seconds of carelessness! Why would God let this happen? Is he punishing me?"

I don't think so. I think, in fact, God was rescuing him. God was trying to get him to see that he was throwing away *eternity* for a few seconds of fame in an athletic arena. Perhaps he needed to lose what he *thought* was valuable so he could gain what is *truly* valuable. Perhaps God put him flat on his back so he would finally look in the right direction, so that he would lean in to hear the voice calling from the burning bush. C. S. Lewis called pain God's "megaphone to rouse a deaf world." He said, "God whispers to us in our pleasures, speaks in our conscience, but shouts in our pains."[5]

The emptiness a person sometimes feels on the other side of achieving a lifelong goal can serve as a burning bush. Years ago, I heard a successful CEO say he spent his whole life climbing the ladder of success only to find upon getting to the top that the ladder was leaning against the wrong building! He's not alone. Many people find that the thing they worked so hard to obtain just didn't deliver what it had promised. In the words of Bono, many people *still haven't found what they're looking for.*

That's because false gods—success, sexual pleasure, power, fame, or even family—always disappoint. The disillusionment on the other side of a fulfilled dream is an invitation to turn aside and hear the voice of the living God.

Reading the Bible may be your burning bush. It was for me. During all the years I silently struggled with my faith, I continued to pour over the Bible. The more I read and pondered, the more I became convinced that the Jesus of the Gospels was *real*. I didn't understand him. Why he did what he did, or didn't do what he didn't do, confused me. But it seemed clear that the God of the Bible was a living, moving being, and that he was calling out—to me. Many who have read the Bible can't escape the idea that it's more than a collection of ancient inspirational stories. I once heard someone describe the experience of reading the Bible like "looking through a keyhole and seeing an eye looking back at you."[6]

Maybe the extraordinary life of some Christian has caused you to wonder if there is more to Jesus than fairy tales and religious chicanery. You wonder how they possess such inner peace, joy, and grace in the vicissitudes of life. I experienced that wonder through my parents. Seeing how real God was to them, how generously they treated people, how joyful they were in struggle and disappointment, and how quickly they ran to God with their problems gave me a glimpse of something I knew had to be real. Their lives made me turn aside and listen.

One of the most effective "evangelists" I've ever known was a young girl with cystic fibrosis, lying in a hospital room, terminally ill. Two years earlier, she had received a double lung transplant but quickly began to experience complications. A few months later, she was diagnosed with a very aggressive kind of cancer. The doctors told her that there was nothing more they could do and that she had less than a year to live. To most, her story seemed devastatingly tragic—a young girl cut down in the prime of her life. But I can't remember ever being in the presence of another person who exuded such consistent serenity and joy. She told the doctors and nurses on her floor and anyone else who would listen that what she was going through was nothing compared to what God had prepared for her in eternity—that our lives, whether we live to be 20 or 120, are only small drops of water compared to the expansive beauty of eternity's ocean. During her last few months, I seemed to meet new people in our church every week impacted by her testimony. Her life was a burning bush that beckoned many to turn aside.

Are you encountering one of these burning bushes now? Have you turned aside to listen?

RESPONDING TO THE INVITATION

One of the most riveting movie scenes I've ever seen is from the 1997 movie *Contact*, starring Jodi Foster and Matthew McConaughey. Dr. Ellie Arroway, played by Foster, is an astronomer who has spent years searching for signs of extraterrestrial life.

After years and years of endless silence, she tunes her sensor to a dark, unexplored sector of deep space.

And then she hears it—the unmistakable sound patterns of communication. Someone was trying to speak. *To her!* The message was focused, deliberate, and personal.

Coming to believe in God is a little bit like that. Not in the "I-hear-alien-voices" sense, but in understanding that a personal and intelligent God is speaking and that he's speaking to you. This realization is a heart-stopping, life-defining moment.

Like I said, faith does not usually begin with the scientific discovery of God but with a recognition that God is speaking. Like Moses, we may not be listening for him when he speaks. But he beckons us to turn aside and consider Jesus, his Voice become flesh, and the inspired record of Jesus's message to humankind, the Bible (John 1:14–18; 2 Tim 3:16–17).

My guess is that you've probably encountered at least one

burning bush in your life. Most likely, several. Maybe you are experiencing one right now.

Recently, a young man showed up at our church on a weekday afternoon. He felt lonely and discouraged about his future. He was not a Christian but felt like God was trying to get his attention and thought the church might help him figure out what to do.

When he showed up, KJ, one of our members, happened to be there, and they began to talk deeply. KJ invited this guy to tag along for the day, and that afternoon they traveled to a place we have downtown that ministers to the less privileged in our city. As they went, they talked through his questions. Before they parted ways, they prayed together. KJ told him he believed that God planted these questions in his heart and that God was working through these questions, doubts, and struggles to draw him closer.

A few days later this young man got an unexpected job offer but didn't have transportation to and from the job. KJ volunteered to drive him until he could make other arrangements. During one of their commutes, the man said he believed God might have arranged all this hardship to call him to surrender his life to God. KJ agreed. KJ explained the gospel to him again, but this man still wasn't ready to go all in.

That next weekend, the young man came to one of our services. Afterward at lunch, he told KJ that the message on Mark 4—which attempted to explain what Jesus is doing in the storms of our life—had addressed every question he was pondering. He said, "KJ, I know God is speaking to me. I can't fight it anymore. I need to listen." So right then, in the middle of Jason's Deli, the man prayed to give his life to Jesus.

God speaks. Constantly. He puts small "speakers" in nature, in beauty, in our pain, our pleasures, and our questions. Most clearly, his voice calls out to us through Scripture.

Are you listening? It might not answer all your questions, but it will bring you face to face with a God even bigger than your questions.

CHAPTER 4

INCOMPREHENSIBLE WISDOM

When I was a seminary student, I heard the tragic story of another seminary student who lost his faith. "Justin" had come to Christ in college through the witness of some of his fraternity brothers. He was smart, articulate, athletic, and popular, and became a Christian leader on campus almost immediately. He started a large, growing Bible study and brought several of his fraternity brothers to Christ. During his senior year, he began to date one of the most popular Christian girls on campus, and by the end of the year they were engaged. That summer, when Justin sensed a call to full-time ministry, no one was surprised.

Justin's meteoric rise continued in seminary. Professors often remarked how insightful he was, and his mentor convinced him to press on toward advanced biblical studies. Everything went well until his final semester. As he worked on his master's thesis, Justin received a phone call from his mom telling him that his dad had filed for separation. Justin was devastated. He had been sharing his new life in Christ with his mom and dad, and he thought they were close to believing.

Shortly after his parents separated, doctors diagnosed Justin's mother with an aggressive stage-four cancer. Justin hoped that, if nothing else, the cancer would draw his parents toward Jesus and bring them back together. But Justin's dad got involved with a younger woman and soon filed for divorce.

It was around this same time that his fiancée unexpectedly broke off their engagement. She offered no real explanation, only that she didn't love him anymore. Justin's whole world was crumbling.

Justin kept asking God why. He knew the seminary answer— God has a good purpose for everything in our lives. He believed God was good, so he prayed for a miracle—in his parents' marriage, with his relationship with his fiancée, and for his mom's health. But his parents never got back together. His fiancée eventually married someone else. Then his mom died. Shortly after the funeral Justin found himself on his face before God screaming, "Why, God? Why aren't you answering my prayers?"

Then a thought occurred to him: "Maybe the reason God hasn't answered my prayers is that he's not actually there." The thought had been hovering there in the back of his mind for quite some time. But in this moment that explanation seemed so compelling—like the only explanation that made sense. Justin stood up and wiped away his tears. In a last, desperate attempt, he opened his Bible and asked God to speak. For over an hour he searched for some verse that would alleviate the pain.

At about 3:00 a.m. he carried his Bible downstairs, set it in a fire pit, doused it with gasoline, and struck the match. He went back upstairs and gathered his master's thesis and several Christian books and burned them too. He described it as his moment of "de-conversion."

The subject of his master's thesis? Old Testament perspectives on pain and suffering.[1]

UNANSWERED QUESTIONS: THE #1 DESTROYER OF FAITH

Maybe you've struggled with questions like Justin's. How can a loving God allow seemingly pointless tragedy? Where was God in the Holocaust? Why isn't God doing more to fix the refugee crisis?

Maybe for you the questions are less philosophical and more personal: Why am *I* suffering? Why won't God fix my parents' marriage?

The inability to understand the "why" of God's ways has been the greatest challenge to faith since the beginning of time. It certainly has been mine.

Bart Ehrman, the notorious agnostic professor of New Testament studies at the University of North Carolina, surprises students every semester when he tells them that what made him lose his faith in seminary was not his problems with the supposed "contradictions in the New Testament" for which he has become famous. Rather, he couldn't understand how a loving God could leave the world in such a broken condition. I once was in the audience when a student asked him, "Is there anything that would cause you to regain your faith?" In response, he quoted a passage from his book, *God's Problem*:

> I think that if, in fact, God Almighty appeared to me and gave me an explanation that could make sense even of the torture, dismemberment, and slaughter of innocent children, and the explanation was so overpowering that I actually could *understand*, then I'd be the first to fall on my knees in humble submission and admiration.[2]

For Ehrman, the problem is not suffering itself; it's suffering for which he can discern no justifiable *purpose*.

Like I said, this problem is certainly not a new one. A good portion of the Bible recounts the confused cries of committed *believers* struggling with God's apparent lack of involvement in their suffering. Men like Moses, Job, David, Jeremiah, Habakkuk, and Paul wrestled with this question with the same bewilderment as Justin and Bart Ehrman.

The basic problem that suffering presents to faith in a good God goes like this, stated first by Epicurus in the fourth century BC:

> If God is all-powerful, he could stop suffering. If he is all-loving, he would want to stop suffering. That purposeless suffering exists shows that God does not exist.

Or the short version of it: If he's good, he would. If he could, he should. That he doesn't means he can't or he won't, which really means that he isn't.

The logic insists that suffering's presence in our world not only brings into question God's wisdom and power, but his very existence.

Slam dunk? No.

Is it a difficult question? Yes. But concluding "God does not exist" is not the only—or even most compelling—answer.

Epicurus's challenge misses a couple crucial and obvious premises: If God is all-powerful and all-loving, then he is also all-wise. And if his wisdom is as far beyond ours as his power is above ours, it shouldn't surprise us that much of his "why" is beyond our immediate ability to understand.

A TRILLION MEGATON BOMBS US. A LIGHTBULB

Think for a minute about how much more powerful than you God must be. As we saw in chapter two, God created at least three septillion one-trillion-megaton-bombs-per-second-energy-producing-exploding-nuclear-spheres with just a word.

My personal ability to generate energy is not nearly as impressive. I have a rowing machine that measures the watts of electricity I produce during an exercise session. I'm not sure what the purpose of that function is other than to humiliate me. Tracking total meters rowed, total calories burned—that makes sense. But do people seriously care about their *wattage* output? As I was thinking about this book, I got the brilliant idea to see how many output watts I could generate giving it everything I had for a two-minute stretch. The result: 320 watts. At least that's what they told me when they revived me. Impressive? That's enough to power five household lightbulbs for about the same amount of time it took you to read the previous page.

Three septillion one-trillion-megaton-bombs-per-second-energy-producing-exploding-nuclear-spheres vs. five energy-efficient lightbulbs for two minutes. And not only did he create all that power, he holds together the universe that contains those stars. I can barely lift the corner of my mattress over my head, and only if I wear a back brace and relax for the rest of the day.

To state the obvious: God's power is immeasurably greater than mine. It doesn't even make sense to compare us. So if the measure of God's *wisdom* is as high above mine as his *power* is above mine, am I really in a place to evaluate it? Would that make any more sense than challenging God to an arm wrestling match? Do I have the perspective required to blow a whistle and call "foul" on God?

Approaching a God of such size and wisdom demands an extraordinary degree of humility, to say the least. Perhaps we should not assume that just because *we* cannot think of a good reason that something bad has happened means that there *cannot* be a good reason.

Philosopher Alvin Plantinga illustrates it like this: If you are asked if there is a camel in your tent, you can determine the answer fairly quickly by glancing inside. If you don't see a camel in your tent, there's not one in there. But if I ask you if there is a *no-see-um* in your tent (for those of you who are from the city, *no-see-ums* are insects whose bite is tremendously irritating but are so small that you, well, can't *"see 'em"*), and you peek inside and conclude that because you don't see any that there are none, that would be foolish. You might wake up the next morning with quite a few itchy bumps to the contrary.

In a similar way, when we say, "I can't believe in God because there is so much *purposeless* evil in the world," we assume that we could immediately perceive whatever purpose is out there. But do we have the perspective and wisdom to declare the absence of any purpose just because we can't see one? Isn't it possible that God might have purposes we can't see yet?

Jacques-Marie-Louis Monsabré, rector of the cathedral in Notre Dame, observed, "If God conceded me his omnipotence for twenty-four hours, I would make many changes in the world. But I know that if he gave me his wisdom, too, I would leave things as they are."[3]

It's ridiculous when you think about it: We imagine a God of omnipotent power but with a brain no bigger than ours—a God with huge, universe-moving muscles and a little itty-bitty, teeny-tiny head.

Solomon sums up our condition rather candidly in the book of Ecclesiastes:

> No one can comprehend [God's work] under the sun. Despite all their efforts to search it out, no one can discover its meaning. Even if the wise claim they know, they cannot really comprehend it (Eccl 8:17).

"No one" is a big category. It includes you and me.

A DIFFICULT PATH TO A GLORIOUS PLACE

When we are in the throes of pain, it is difficult to feel assured of God's wisdom and love. But if God is as big as Scripture says he is (and as big as creation itself demands!), then our inability to perceive his purpose doesn't mean there's not one at work. Our inability to discern God's purpose has more to do with how limited our perspective is.

When my first child turned one, we took her in for a round of shots. They should require some kind of parent-debriefing before child immunizations because, as hard as it was for her, I was the one who almost didn't make it. The doctor asked me to hold my little girl on my lap as she stuck a needle in her arm four different times. Each time, my daughter let out a scream that could have woken the dead. What was worse, though, was how frantically she looked around the room searching for help. When her eyes found mine, it was clear she expected me to do something to stop this cruel doctor. But there I sat—not only not stopping the doctor, but helping her!

She couldn't understand *why* the one who loved her was not helping her. She couldn't perceive that I was doing what I was doing *because* I loved her and not *in spite* of it.

Isn't it possible that the pain that God allows us to go through might be like that too? Just as those painful shots produced a healthier life for my daughter, might it be that our pain in life yields a much greater and happier eternity?

The apostle Paul compares our journey in this life to the process of childbirth: temporary pain for long-term joy. I have watched my wife give birth to each of our four children. I've seen the very real pain she went through. One of them came so fast we weren't even able to get the epidural—we barely made it through the hospital door! Each labor period, though relatively brief in the grand scheme of things, was real, intense, and agonizing. But when we held each of our newborn children, the pain was all but forgotten. And now, that pain seems like nothing more than a distant memory.

Paul said, "I consider that our present sufferings are not worth comparing with the glory that will be revealed in us. . . . We know that the whole creation has been groaning as in the pains of childbirth right up to the present time" (Rom 8:18, 22).

"*Not worth comparing*." Paul is not saying the pain isn't real. It is. He's saying that something so awesome is coming that the worst pain we experience now can't even be compared to it. Mother Teresa, intimately acquainted with great suffering, said that once we enter eternity the worst things we experienced on earth will seem like "one bad night in a cheap hotel."

That's not to minimize, trivialize, or explain away our pain now, but to enlarge our expectation and hope of what God has prepared for us in eternity. "What no eye has seen," Paul said, "'what no ear has heard, and what no human mind has conceived'—the things God has prepared for those who love him" (1 Cor 2:9).

A friend and father of three that I know was diagnosed with a rare and aggressive form of brain cancer. Doctors told him initially that his chances of survival were not good. He is praying, as are many of us, for a complete and total healing. But he said something the other day that brought it all into perspective: "When we get to heaven, it's not that we look back and see the reasons bad things happen and say, 'Oh ... *that's* why that happened!' Rather, we will say, '*What* bad things?' In that moment, we will be so consumed with God and our future in him that we will scarcely remember the process he used!"

Scripture tells us that a day is coming when God will undo every injustice and heal every hurt and that his end "product" will be stronger and better for having gone through the process. On that day God will wipe away every tear, says the apostle John, and make all things new (Rev 21:4–5). To use the words of J. R. R. Tolkien in *The Lord of the Rings*, he will "make every sad thing come untrue." God doesn't erase our memory of them; he shows us how they were all part of a beautiful plan. The truth of their destructiveness is overwritten by the truth of his redemption.

One of my favorite promises about this wonderful day is found in Isaiah:

> This is what the Sovereign LORD says:
> "[In that day], I will give a signal to the godless nations.
> They will carry your little sons back to you in their arms;
> they will bring your daughters on their shoulders."
> (Isa 49:22 NLT)

The slave who watched his family torn apart by injustice will one day see them reunited again. The couple who lost their five-year-old son to tuberculosis will have him brought back on the shoulders of angels. What a day that will be!

God uses pain to prepare his people for that future, like a doctor who gives shots to improve your quality of life or a coach who presses you to the point of exhaustion to strengthen your endurance. Our current world may not be the best place we can imagine, but it is *the* world best suited to bring us to *that* best world. God's plan is not just to take us to heaven; it is to put heaven into us.

Once you understand that, you'll interpret the pain in your life differently. C. S. Lewis said, "If you think of this world as a place intended simply for our happiness, you find it quite intolerable: think of it as a place of training and correction and it's not so bad."[4]

Sometimes we can see what God is doing. You can probably look back on some painful period of your life and see how the difficulty made you better. The illness helped you reexamine your priorities. The breakup helped you regain your self-confidence. Getting passed over for a promotion kept you from destroying your family. So here's the thing: if already, with limited time and perspective, we can see some of God's good purposes in our pain, don't you think, given infinite time and perspective, we'll see a reason for all of it? That's not something we should expect to see fully on earth. No one, Solomon says, can comprehend God's work while they live "under the sun" (Eccl 8:17). Our earthly minds are just not big enough.

GOD'S BOOK OF SECRETS

God tells us that while we live on earth, some things about his plan will remain a secret: "The secret things belong to the LORD our God, but the things revealed belong to us and to our children forever, that we may follow all the words of this law" (Deut 29:29).

Not knowing all of God's secrets drives Type-A, figure-everything-out people (like me) crazy. Yet Moses tells us that God has structured the universe so that we'll *never* figure some things out this side of eternity.

That means if we make our faith contingent on being able to figure everything out, we'll never believe. It's not that if you'll just read one more book, attend one more lecture, or meditate on one more truth that it will all at last make sense. It's literally impossible, God says, on this side of heaven to understand *all* that he is doing.

I'm not urging you to adopt a blind, naïve faith. I'm just saying that *if* God does indeed exist, he surely is a God of incomprehensible wisdom, and we should approach him as such—assuming that some of what he does lies beyond our grasp. Don't flatter yourself; you can't engage in a battle of wits with the One who fashioned your brain.

We know that Moses, who wrote these things about God, had his own unanswered questions. At the end of his life, Moses was forbidden from entering the promised land because he lost his temper one afternoon, smashing his staff into the rock to draw water from it rather than speaking to it like God had commanded (Num 20:7–12). For that, he was forbidden entry into the promised land after forty years of faithful leadership. What he did was wrong, but I still sympathize with Moses. The Israelites were acting like spoiled toddlers. I would have probably gone "Old Testament" on them long before Moses did and used that stick on far more than the rock's face.

Did Moses see this as a fitting punishment? We don't know, but I have a hard time seeing how he could have. He had been ready to go into the land forty years prior. It was the *Israelites'* lack of faith that kept him out the first time.

Even so, Moses did not cross out or asterisk all the things he had written about God's faithfulness and steadfast love. Instead, he composed a new song about them, a song that the book of Revelation says we will sing with him throughout eternity:

> Great and marvelous are your deeds,
>   Lord God Almighty.
> *Just and true* are your ways,
>   King of the nations. (Rev 15:3, emphasis mine)

Moses declared that God's ways were altogether true and righteous even when he couldn't understand them. He knew the God who had spoken to him out of the bush was the I AM of perfect truth and justice.

THE ANSWER BEHIND ALL OTHER ANSWERS

Job was another man of faith who had a lot of questions for God, questions he thought deserved answers. And God eventually answered him, just not like Job expected. He answered by asking Job some questions of his own:

> Where were you when I laid the earth's foundation? . . .
> What is the way to the abode of light?
> And where does darkness reside? (Job 38:4, 19)

And forty more questions like these. In other words, "Job, are you and I really on level playing fields? I tell you what, Job. Let's meet for coffee to discuss your objections to my methods. You bring your universe and I'll bring mine, and we'll compare. . . . Oh, what's that? You don't have a universe? Then maybe you're not in a place to judge how I rule mine."

Imagine a seven-year-old on a field trip visiting Cape Canaveral to observe a rocket launch. And the child begins lecturing the rocket scientist about why the rocket won't fly: "That rocket is too heavy. It's the wrong shape. It needs wings." The scientist might try to explain to him why he is wrong, but it's unlikely that the child will understand. Instead, the scientist might simply say, "Um, no, son. Sit back and watch." The scientist's ability to *do* invalidates the challenge from the child. That's essentially how God answers Job.

God's answer to Job's queries is not really an answer; it's a display. "Job, if you can't even understand the *natural* world, can you really expect to understand the purposes of the *eternal* God above it?"

Ironically, we who read the book of Job know even more than Job understood about the reasons for his suffering! At the beginning of the book the narrator explained that one of God's primary purposes in Job's suffering was to prove to the angels that God was worthy of being worshiped for himself apart from any of his good gifts (Job 1–2). Job's suffering was a display for the angels. But God doesn't tell Job this. He simply answers Job by showing Job how big he is.

Sometimes that is all he gives us too.

I am not saying that we can never hope to understand the reason for some of our suffering. Just as there was a reason for Job's suffering, there is a reason for ours, and sometimes God shows us what that is. Nor am I saying that there is no place for questioning God. Psalms is *filled* with people who do just that, sometimes with disturbing honesty. So yes, ask God your questions. But as you do so, do it with a proper posture toward the One you are addressing.

God said to Isaiah,

> For my thoughts are not your thoughts,
>> neither are your ways my ways, declares the LORD.
> For as the heavens are higher than the earth,
>> so are my ways higher than your ways
>> and my thoughts than your thoughts. (Isa 55:8–9, ESV)

We know even more now than Isaiah did about how much higher the stars are above us. That's how much higher God's wisdom is than ours.

Do we dare flatter ourselves by believing that we could understand everything if God would just take a minute to explain it to us?

REVELATION, NOT EXPLANATION

As I said, if our faith is conditioned on understanding everything, we'll never believe. God often provides no *explanation* for his ways. Instead, he gives us a *revelation* of his character.

God let Job know that his Redeemer lived, even in the darkest days of his suffering, and assured Job that he would stand victoriously on earth with that Redeemer someday (Job 19:25). In Job's bitterest moments, he discovered God walking with him through the pain, and he knew that one day his Redeemer would weave it together into a beautiful story of victory that eclipsed the pain.

In many cases, we have to live out our days not knowing the precise reason for terrible events. But the cross shows us what they *cannot* mean. They cannot mean that God is absent or out of control.

At the cross, we see God willingly enter into our suffering. There he did more than promise to fix our pain; he immersed himself in it. And there we see that even when things looked like they were out of control, they really weren't. If there ever were a time when it looked like God had lost control, it was on the day Jesus was crucified! Evil, it seemed, had triumphed at last. Now, however, we realize that there had never been a time when God was more *in* control. In the cross, he took the worst atrocity in human history—the murder of his Son—and turned it for his glory and our good.

Isn't it possible that God is doing that same thing now in your pain?

The cross both reveals God's intentions *for* the world and gives us insight into *how* he accomplishes them. He works in all things for his glory and our salvation.

Exactly what God is doing in *particular* situations may remain a secret, but what he is doing through *all* of them is not. He is making us love Jesus more and look more like him (Rom 8:28–29). He is preparing us for endless joy and pleasure (Ps 16:11). Sometimes we may not be able to see the silver lining behind the dark cloud. But the cross is the evidence that it's there. Even in the darkness, we know our Redeemer lives.

King David, suffering through a dark chapter of his own, expressed his faith in the character of God with these words—words that have brought solace to my heart during some of my darkest and most confusing hours:

My heart is not proud, LORD,
    my eyes are not haughty;
I do not concern myself with great matters
    or things too wonderful for me.
But I have calmed and quieted myself,
    I am like a weaned child with its mother;
    like a weaned child I am content.
Israel, put your hope in the LORD
    both now and forevermore. (Ps 131)

Some things were simply "too wonderful" for David to understand, too "great" for his small mind. So during the pain, he clung tightly to the God who cared for him more than a new mother cares for her infant child. We may not understand all our Father's ways, but we know him. The cross reveals him. Even where we can't trace his hand, we can trust his heart.

Sometimes, from the depths of confusion, pain, or loss, we must simply gaze at the cross and empty tomb of Jesus and say,

'Tis so sweet to trust in Jesus;
just to take him at his word;
just to rest upon his promise;
just to know, 'Thus says the Lord!'

Jesus, Jesus, how I trust him!
How I've proved him o'er and o'er;
Jesus, Jesus, precious Jesus!
Oh, for grace, to trust him more![5]

Let me be clear: I still don't understand everything God is doing in my life, and I probably won't until I meet Jesus face to face. What I do know is that God has revealed his intentions for me clearly in the cross of Jesus.

God is too big for me to base my trust in him on my ability to figure him out. I trust him because I know that my Redeemer lives.

I have no doubt that when I look back on history from the vantage point of eternity, I'll see that he was infinitely worthy of that trust.

What I'll surely be confused by in eternity is how a God of such infinite power and purity could have loved me. Scripture, after all, presents him as a God of unblemished purity. The greatest mystery of the universe is how we, a corrupted and traitorous race, can still hope to spend eternity in his presence. This is where most people diminish God—where their God is not God enough—so we'll turn our attention there next.

CHAPTER 5

UNTOUCHABLE HOLINESS

N o sir," my terrified friend told his dad. "I haven't called any dirty phone numbers."

"Son," his dad said, "I know you are lying. I just hit redial on the phone, and the line connected to a pornographic phone service."

The day before, one of the eighth graders at my friend's school had given him a "1–900" phone number. If you were born after 1985 you might not know what a "1–900" number is. You could dial them for information, services, or "entertainment." They always came with a hefty charge.

My friend lived a pretty protected life, so he had no idea what a "1–900" number was. He was so alarmed by what he heard the prerecorded female voice saying on the other end of the line that he hung up. But then he picked up the receiver and dialed again, this time listening all the way through. He picked up the phone a third time to call a friend and say, "Hey, you need to hear this." By the time Saturday morning rolled around, he and his friends had called the number fifty-eight times.

Confronted with his lie, my friend panicked and burst into tears: "Yes, Daddy, you are right. A kid gave that number to me at school, and I didn't know what it was, so I called it . . . and, oh Dad . . .

it was the scariest woman I've ever heard in my life. I hung up on her immediately. I'm sorry, Daddy, I won't ever do that again."

His dad, trusting him, said, "Well, Son, that's a hard lesson to learn. But I'm proud of how you handled it."

Relieved, my friend thought he had dodged the bullet.

Unfortunately, his understanding of how the world worked did not yet include the concept of a phone bill. Soon enough, it would.

A few weeks later, he was summoned to the principal's office. There he was informed that his mom was waiting for him in the parking lot. When he went out to the car and asked his mom what was going on, she said nothing and simply pointed to a bill from the phone company for nearly $500.00. There, on paper, was a detailed record of every single one of his fifty-eight calls.

If you're like me, you probably don't know whether to laugh or cry at that story. Pornography is no joking matter. But I share that story because most of us know what it's like to fear the exposure of some part of our lives that we'd rather keep hidden. Imagine how horrifying it would be if everyone knew everything about you or if they could see, displayed on a little monitor, whatever went through your mind at any given moment.

Has something ever slipped out of your mouth that you immediately wished you could take back? Maybe it was something said in anger, an unkind comment about a friend, or the verbalization of some inappropriate desire. And perhaps you returned to the person you said it to, embarrassed, and said something like, *"I'm sorry. I don't know why I said that. That's not really me."* Yet . . . in that moment it was you, wasn't it? In that moment, it was exactly how you felt. It actually was from the real you—the you that you usually filter.

But just because we filter effectively doesn't mean the impure thought isn't there. A lot of things stay buried in our hearts until the right set of circumstances evoke them.

The writer of Hebrews tells us that one day every thought, word, and deed will be laid bare, naked, and exposed before God (Heb

4:13). What will that moment be like? It will probably feel a lot like my eighth-grade friend staring at his phone bill. But a billion times worse.

The prophet Isaiah found himself in exactly this position, and it changed how he thought of himself—and how he approached God—forever.

INDESCRIBABLY HOLY

Isaiah had gotten off to a pretty good start in ministry. He had a good reputation and was making quite a name for himself. He was one of Israel's premier preachers. But one day Isaiah had an encounter he was not ready for. He found himself face to face with the God he claimed to represent:

> In the year that King Uzziah died, I saw the Lord, high and exalted, seated on a throne; and the train of his robe filled the temple. Above him were seraphim, each with six wings: With two wings they covered their faces, with two they covered their feet, and with two they were flying. And they were calling to one another:
>
> > "Holy, holy, holy is the LORD Almighty;
> > the whole earth is full of his glory!"
>
> At the sound of their voices the doorposts and thresholds shook and the temple was filled with smoke.
> "Woe to me!" I cried. "I am ruined! For I am a man of unclean lips, and I live among a people of unclean lips, and my eyes have seen the King, the LORD Almighty." (Isa 6:1–5)

Stop for a moment and try to take in this scene, if you can. Two angels, which Isaiah literally calls *burning ones* ("seraphim"), hover over God's throne, calling back and forth to each other, "Holy, holy, holy." These angels, by the way, are not the chubby, toddler-like winged three-year-olds you might see on a Valentine's card, sauntering about heaven in diapers with toy bows and arrows. Nor do they carry themselves like the genteel, bumbling old men depicted in movies like *It's a Wonderful Life*. They are magnificently powerful, terrifying creatures. Every time someone encounters one in Scripture, the angel's first words are, "Wait, don't die!" because whoever sees the angel assumes that is what is about to happen.

These radiant beings hover in reverent fear before the throne of God. Of their six wings, they use four to cover their faces and feet and two to fly. Their bodies pulsate with divine energy, and their hearts burn with white-hot worship as they proclaim the holiness of God: "Holy, holy, holy."

Repeating "holy" three times is not merely poetic. In Hebrew, repetition expresses superlative. If something is really big, you say it is "big, big," or if a lake is very deep, you say it is "deep, deep." "Holy, holy, holy" is the *only* superlative in the Bible with a threefold repetition.[1] God *exists* as infinite, undiluted holiness.

Even the pillars of the temple tremble in his presence.

The angels Isaiah sees stand continually before God's throne proclaiming God's holiness to each other. This means that as you read these words the angels are still hovering, calling out God's holiness. When you put this book down, they will remain, with millions of others. When you go to bed tonight, they will continue, and when you wake up, they will still be going. They do this perpetually for eternity.

Overwhelmed by God's glory, Isaiah cries out in despair: "Woe is me! For I am lost; for I am a man of unclean lips, and I dwell in the midst of a people of unclean lips; for my eyes have seen the King, the LORD of hosts!" (Isa 6:5 ESV).

Isaiah learned two things about himself that forever changed his theology: his goodness was not that good, and his strengths were not that strong.

HIS GOODNESS WAS NOT THAT GOOD

Nearly 90 percent of Americans think that they are "above average" when it comes to morality.[2] That definitely indicts our math ability, but it also shows us that most people feel, deep down, that they are pretty good. Typically, we measure our goodness by contrasting ourselves with others. We know we're not perfect, but we're not as bad as *that person* or *those people*. As long as God grades on a curve, we figure we'll be OK.

Take note. When Isaiah had his vision of encountering the presence of God, he didn't find himself in a lineup with other sinners. He found himself face to face with *God*. His conclusion was not "I am above average." It was "I am *lost*." Ruined. Doomed.

We might wonder if Isaiah overreacted. After all, he was a respected prophet. But his despair was fully justified when you consider what happened to others in the Bible who found themselves in the unfiltered presence of God's holiness:

Uzzah reached out his hand to steady the ark so it didn't fall into the dirt as a group of oxen pulled it along the road. God struck him dead. For *one* forbidden touch (2 Sam 6:7)!

Lot's wife was turned into a pillar of salt for taking *one* look at the city God told her to flee. She lost her life for *one* glance (Gen 19:26).

A group of seventy Israelites peered with curiosity into the ark of the covenant, which housed God's presence. God killed all seventy. For *one* forbidden look (1 Sam 6:19).

The book of Numbers records the story of a man who, right after the giving of the law, broke the law by collecting sticks on the Sabbath. The people brought him to God to ask what the punishment should be. *God* said, "Stone him." For *one* small infraction of the law of God that most of us would consider to be morally innocuous, this man lost his life (Num 15:32–36).

In the Garden of Eden, one bite from the forbidden fruit brought condemnation on the entire human race. Think about that: every disease, every famine, every natural disaster—eternal punishment—came about as the result of *one* bite from the forbidden fruit (Gen 3:1–24).[3]

One act of disobedience qualifies us for eternal separation.

Isaiah offers up no excuses. What could he possibly say to hide or excuse his defilement? No wonder he despaired. What hope do *any* of us have before God?

INFINITE, PURE, PERFECT HOLINESS

Lest you think that this is merely the cranky, judgmental Old Testament God—God in his middle school years—who morphs into a much nicer and more flexible deity in the New Testament—Jesus, the meek and mild—consider what happened to the New Testament couple Ananias and Sapphira when they lied one Sunday about a church offering. They exaggerated the amount they gave, and God struck them dead (Acts 5:1–11).

Thankfully, God hasn't done that to every person who has lied in church. But in their story God gives us a glimpse of his attitude toward sin so that we consider what it will be like for all of us one day when we stand exposed before God. Are you ready for that moment when all your secrets and hidden thoughts are exposed?

We tend to think of sin as "not that bad" because we think of it only in terms of how it affects other humans. We think, "Well, I haven't killed anybody, so how bad could my sin actually be?" Sin's "wickedness," however, comes from its offensiveness toward *God*. The wickedness of any deed is measured, at least in part, by the nature of the one it is directed against. If you get mad and kick a wall, you might have to pay for the wall, but that's it. Do the same thing to a dog, however, and people will think you've done a genuinely bad thing and probably not let their kids play with your kids. Do it to the lady next to you in the grocery store, and you'll go to jail. Walk into Buckingham Palace and attempt to roundhouse the queen of England, and you probably won't see daylight for a long, long time.

What about sin against the *infinitely* glorious God? How can we even begin to describe the wickedness of rebelling against him? Sin against the *infinite* holiness of God is infinitely wicked and deserves infinite punishment.

Perhaps you say, "But don't we do a lot of good things too? What about the guy who throws himself on a grenade to save his buddy, or the single mom who sacrifices everything to give her kids a chance at a better life?" Those are indeed genuinely good things, but they don't remove the wickedness of our rebellion.

Imagine observing two terrorists planning the bombing of an elementary school. In the midst of their planning, they take a lunch break, and one realizes his companion doesn't have any lunch so he shares his with him. That's a genuinely good thing, right? But in light of the larger context—who they are and what they are about to do—it's difficult to call that good thing "good."

What if our rebellion to God was the same way in God's sight, but infinitely worse? Goodness done in the context of cosmic treason still seems wicked.

Standing before God's throne, Isaiah realized that he was charged with treason of the highest order. He had joined Satan in his rebellion against God's authority. That sin now corrupted every single part of his life. It infected his mouth, defiling every word he spoke—even the religious ones.

The prophet Habakkuk says that God is of such purity that he cannot even look at evil (Hab 1:13). He is so perfectly good that injustice, impurity, or unkindness of any kind, even in the smallest amounts, cannot survive in his presence. Suppose you are getting a blood transfusion and you find out that 1 percent of it was contaminated with HIV. Would it help if the nurse said, "Don't worry; it's only 1 percent"? "No!" we'd shout back, "There is no such thing as *only* 1 percent! One speck contaminates the whole lot." The revulsion we would feel at such a thought is just a fraction of what God feels in the presence of our sin. Our sin is more dangerous than HIV. It's more harmful than the most aggressive cancer. It's more offensive than the most heinous acts of wickedness we've seen on the news.

The majesty of God's holiness means that there is no such thing as "just a little sin." Coming into his presence with even a single sin is like a piece of wax paper touching the surface of the sun.

That's why God struck Uzzah dead when he touched the ark. Uzzah thought he was doing a favor for God by keeping the ark from falling, but he thought too little of the holiness of God. His sin-stained hand was far filthier than the dirt the ark would have landed upon. The dirt had never rebelled against God. Uzzah had.

Sin makes us detestable to a holy God. And our lives are saturated with it.

AM I RUINED?

God gave us a way to evaluate the spiritual health of our hearts: the Ten Commandments. Have you ever considered how you measure up against them? I have, and when I read through them, I begin to feel the same despair Isaiah felt.

When I stand to teach God's Word, I often catch myself wondering if people are impressed with *me*. That's a violation of the first commandment, caring more about my glory than God's.

I can think of countless times where I bent the truth to get out of an uncomfortable situation. Or exaggerated the truth to make myself look better. In both cases, my dishonesty is an attempt to bolster my reputation, which means I am not only breaking the ninth commandment to not bear falsehood, but also the first, by caring about other people's opinions more than I do God's.

Throughout my life, I have resisted the God-ordained authorities in my life—whether my parents, teachers, traffic cops, or the

IRS. This is a violation of the fifth commandment. By flouting God-ordained authorities in my life, I am flouting *his* authority.

I may never have committed adultery, but Jesus said that if we look on someone who is not our spouse and indulge in lustful thoughts about them, we are guilty of adultery before God. I don't know a single person alive who can claim they have never done that.

I fail at the rest of the Ten Commandments in similar ways. Now, I know what you might be saying: "Murder! Get to murder. I'm clear on that one." Not so fast. Jesus said that hatred toward others is the essence of a murderous spirit. You may not act on it, but the spirit of murder is still in you. I think about how often I resent those who are better than me at something, even fantasizing about something bad happening to them: The best athlete on my basketball team air-balling a foul shot. The best-looking guy contracting an odorous fungal-acne outbreak. A more successful pastor having problems in his church. A more successful writer being raked over the coals by other bloggers. Those who delight in the misfortune of others are regarded as murderers before God (Matt 5:21–22).

When it's all tallied up, I'm zero for ten on commandments. And yet it's with this heart that I expect to enter the presence of God. If you get a zero on the final exam, you're not going to pass the class.

After encountering the holiness of God, Isaiah said of his best deeds, *"All our righteous acts are like filthy rags"* (Isa 64:6). The word he uses for "filthy" literally means "defiled." Jews in that day used the term to refer to things that were not just dirty, but contagious, diseased, or ceremonially unclean. A leper's rags were "filthy." Isaiah imagines himself coming into God's presence and laying down his "good deeds" at God's feet as a pile of contaminated, diseased rags, each one soaked through with the pus and gore of sin. I look into my own heart and know he is right. My hearth is filthy.

This doesn't mean we have never done anything that pleases God. It just means that if we are depending on the purity of our deeds to buy our way into heaven, we are fools.

Even when I do obey the commandments, reflecting on my struggle to obey shows me how much trouble I'm in! If I truly loved God, I wouldn't *need* to be commanded to do righteous things. It shouldn't be a struggle. I don't need to be commanded to do the things I really love. You never have to command me to eat a steak, take a nap, hug my kids, or kiss my wife. So why do I need to be commanded to love God, love people, and act righteously? What's wrong with my heart that it needs to be *commanded* to do these things?

It's my heart that is the problem.

I need more than instructions on how to be righteous. I need a heart change.

No wonder Isaiah, when he came face to face with the holiness of God, said, "Woe is me! I am lost." His sense of his own "goodness" had been totally obliterated.

As Gregory Koukl says, "Absolute goodness makes God absolutely dangerous, for the only ones who are safe are the ones who are good like he is."[4]

HIS STRENGTHS WERE NOT THAT STRONG

In God's presence, not only did Isaiah see that his goodness was not that good, he saw that his strengths were not that strong. Isaiah specifically bemoans the filthiness of *his lips*. A prophet's "lips" were his trade. He would have felt about his mouth the way a pianist feels about her fingers, or the way a quarterback feels about his arm. But in God's presence, Isaiah declares even those strengths worthless.[5]

The King James Version of the Bible translates what Isaiah said as "Woe is me! for I am undone." I think that translation probably better carries what Isaiah was trying to say. In the presence of God, Isaiah felt like he was literally *coming apart at the seams*. The "glue" that held his life together—his goodness, his accomplishments, his strengths—he now found utterly worthless. What did he have left?

His goodness was a sham and his strengths were worthless. What else of worth did he have to hold onto?

The apostle Paul records a similar experience. As a Jewish leader, Paul prided himself on his obedience to the law. He kept it better than anyone he knew. But one day as he meditated on the tenth commandment, "You shall not covet," he realized that he had always wanted more—*more success, more fame, more power, more recognition.* What he had was never enough (Rom 7:9). He began to realize that all his supposed "righteousness" was, in reality, "dung" (KJV) or "garbage" (NIV). Actually, the word Paul uses in Philippians 3:8 is *scubala*, the kind of word your parents would have grounded you for using. In the light of God's holiness, Paul saw even the praiseworthy things on which he had proudly based his identity to be a disgusting pile of *scubala*.

Each of us has something that defines us, some strength that we believe holds our lives together. What is it for you?

Here's a way of figuring that out: When you're worried about your future, to what do you look to tell yourself that things will be okay? Your talents? "Even if I lose it all, I can rebuild." Your family? "As long as we have each other, we'll be fine." Your morality? "At least I'm a decent person. Good always wins in the end." Your wealth? "We can weather this storm. We have plenty in savings."

We can truly know God only when we see that everything else we rely on—our intelligence, our virtue, our possessions, our religion, and even our relationships—are worthless in our pursuit to understand, please, and serve the only one who matters.

Thus, God's gracious work in us begins, as it did with Isaiah and Paul, by leading us to despair. Just as Job had to realize the smallness of his mind in order to receive the wisdom of God, so Isaiah had to realize the filthiness of his heart to embrace the grace of God.

God doesn't reveal our sins and our shortcomings in order to embarrass or humiliate us. Quite the opposite. He wants us to know his love, the greatest treasure in the universe, and it's not until we see how sinful and incapacitated we are that God can introduce us to that love. Despair leads us to a new hope, a hope found in his grace and not in our goodness. As John Stott says, "We can cry 'Hallelujah' with authenticity only after we have cried 'Woe is me, for I am lost.'"[6]

REDEEMED TO A NEW HOPE

Thankfully, Isaiah's encounter did not end in a cry of despair. Just when Isaiah thought he was doomed, one of the angels descended, took a glowing coal from the altar, and flew toward Isaiah's face. At first, Isaiah probably thought the angel was going to kill him. But instead the angel touched Isaiah's lips with the burning coal and said, "See, this has touched your lips; your guilt is taken away and your sin atoned for" (Isa 6:7). Instead of bringing destruction, the fire of God's holiness healed him. How can this be?

A coal is what remains after a fire has burned itself out. The angel took the blood-soaked coal from the altar where sacrifices for sin had been offered, showing Isaiah that the fire of judgment for his sin had been burned out on a substitute.

In an instant, without the slightest effort on his part, Isaiah's guilt was gone. He stood safe in the presence of infinite holiness. A lamb had been "ruined" in his place.[7]

Isaiah later prophesied, in great detail, about another sacrificial Lamb that would die in the place of sinners, the blood-soaked coals of whose sacrifice would bring healing to all who received it. He says this coming Lamb

> was pierced for our transgressions,
>   he was crushed for our iniquities;
> the punishment that brought us peace was on him,
>   and by his wounds we are healed.
> We all, like sheep, have gone astray,
>   each of us has turned to our own way;

and the Lord has laid on him
the iniquity of us all. (Isa 53:5–6)

Jesus was the Lamb who died in our place so we can stand without fear in the presence of an infinitely holy God.

Jesus, you see, had an experience very similar to that of Isaiah. In the garden of Gethsemane, Jesus came face to face with the holiness of God. Although his lips were pure, he wrapped himself in *our* filthy rags. No angel came, however, with a coal to cleanse his lips because he was the Lamb sent to die in the fires of judgment in our place.

What Isaiah feared and deserved—death—Jesus took in his place. Now we can come boldly before God's throne with no fear of judgment (Rom 8:1; Heb 4:16).

Isaiah's hope for knowing God was not found in his goodness or strengths, nor in the hope that God would grade on a curve. His hope was found in God's extravagant grace toward him in Jesus. That's where we must find our hope too.

We typically deal with our imperfections by trying to minimize the holiness of God. We assert that our sin is not *that* bad, and God is not *that* offended by it. Scripture, however, tells us the opposite. Our sin was *that* bad—so bad, in fact, that the perfect Son of God had to die to remove it. But he is so gracious that he was *glad* to do it.

We can know God like Isaiah knew him if we place our hope in his grace, not in our goodness. We'll never be able to crawl upwards to him. We can't be good enough to earn his approval or smart enough to figure him out. We have to receive him just as he offers himself: in grace. The fear of God precedes the knowledge of God. Always.

Through the apostle Paul, God says,

For it is written:
"I will destroy the wisdom of the wise;
the intelligence of the intelligent I will frustrate."

> Where is the wise person? Where is the teacher of the law? Where is the philosopher of this age? Has not God made foolish the wisdom of the world? For since in the wisdom of God the world through its wisdom did not know him, God was pleased through the foolishness of what was preached to save those who believe. (1 Cor 1:19–21)

The incredible news of the gospel is that while God's holiness demands perfection, his love was gracious enough to supply it for us through a substitute.

If we cover our sin, God will expose it in judgment. If we rely on our strength, God will abandon us to weakness. If we boast in our wisdom, God will leave us in darkness. But if we expose our sin to Jesus—in all its inglorious ugliness—he will cover it with his extravagant grace. If we confess our weakness, he will fill us with his strength. If we admit our foolishness, he will bestow his wisdom upon us. If we allow ourselves to be undone in his presence, he will piece us back together in love.

CONFIDENCE THAT STANDS AGAINST THE WORLD

This may be jumping too far ahead, but I can't help myself. (Consider this an appetizer for what you'll experience later in this book.) Confessing our inability to God gives us an incredible *confidence* before him. It does so because the source of our confidence shifts from our *limited* ability to his *infinite* willingness. Isaiah left his encounter with God's holiness a changed man. His writing takes on a different character. His preaching becomes personal and passionate, and he gained the courage to stand against the whole world.

At the end of this encounter, God recommissioned Isaiah into ministry with these words:

Go and tell this people:

> "Be ever hearing, but never understanding;
>   be ever seeing, but never perceiving.'
> Make the heart of this people calloused;
>   make their ears dull
>   and close their eyes." (Isa 6:9–10)

On the one hand, that's *not* an encouraging prognosis. "Isaiah, for the rest of your life people are going to misunderstand and malign you." And that's exactly what happened. Jewish history tells us that Isaiah died by being put inside a log and sawn in two. But Isaiah went into this frightening future undaunted because he was now more confident in the God who stood behind him than he was afraid of the dangers that lay before him.

That kind of confidence comes from only one place: basing your hope on God's grace and not on yourself. Trusting in his wisdom and not your intellect. Relying on his strength and not your ability.

When my oldest daughter was five, I was amazed by how often she would notice planes in the sky. "Look, Dad! Way up there—a plane!" she would say. I wondered how she always knew they were there when I hadn't seen or heard anything.

One day the answer occurred to me. At three-foot-four she was always looking up. Everything in the world was "up" to her! And because she was always looking up, she saw what was high above both of us.

The people who see and know God are those whose sense of smallness, unworthiness, and inability always causes them to look upward toward his holiness, trusting in his incredible promises of grace and not in their abilities to figure him out but his willingness to reveal himself.

Seeing your weakness and sinfulness before God is a good thing. It's the beginning of an experience of grace. It's the beginning of knowledge of God. As Billy Graham says, "When we have come to the end of ourselves, we find the beginning of God."

This encounter calls for a very specific response, and whether you respond that way is the most important decision you will ever make.

CHAPTER 6

ONE CHOICE

When Moses encountered the burning bush, he had some legitimate questions. He wondered where God had been for the last four hundred years while Israel suffered. He wondered why God let him fail so miserably the first time he tried to rescue Israel. Now he wondered how God could use someone so broken to liberate a nation from the strongest empire in the world.

God did not answer a single one. To Moses's doubts, he simply said, "I AM."

If God truly is the I AM, that's the only thing that matters.

To challenge *what* the Voice says—to argue against the wisdom of the I AM—is a bit like my youngest son refusing to obey my instructions when I tell him not to put a fork into those little slots on the wall. To him, fork + electrical socket = perfect fit. But I know more than he does. So when my son asks, "*Why* can't I do that, Dad?" I could, of course, divulge insights about the principles of electricity: "Well, Son, miles away from here a giant turbine stimulates the electrons in an atom sequence in a way that makes these subatomic particles called electrons jump into the circuits of other atoms, creating a polar imbalance which leads to chain reaction that produces what we call 'electricity.' And while toaster ovens and washing machines need this chain reaction to function, if you

85

encounter too much of it directly, it will overload the synapses of your central nervous system, and they will cease to function, rendering you dead." Instead, I opt for a much simpler line: "Don't do that, Son." He doesn't have the full capacity to understand everything yet, so for now I ask for his trust. Few would say this is poor or lazy parenting.

Maybe you object: "But we're not children." Yes, but which is greater: the gap between my adolescent son's understanding of the world and mine, or the gap between my understanding and God's? Is it unfair that God sometimes simply asks for our trust?

No matter how many questions Moses had, there was only one pertinent question: Did the voice belong to God? Faith isn't a blind leap in the dark. It's not a sentimental feeling that everything will turn out alright in the end. It is a choice to *trust* the Voice of God because it belongs to I AM. Moses could have dismissed the whole experience as a mirage and walked away. Did the voice really belong to God?

This is the question each of us is presented with: Does "the Voice" in Scripture really belong to God?

IS JESUS WHO HE SAID HE WAS?

Within a fifty-mile radius of where I live, 150,000 college students attend one of our region's universities, and about 2,000 of those students call our church home.

College students add a lot to our church. Money, of course, is not one of them. The first weekend college students first started coming to our church, three showed up, and the next weekend three hundred showed up—riding in the same two cars. During that month our attendance tripled, and our average weekly giving went up $13.48. One of my most cherished memories as a pastor is the Sunday an usher brought me an offering plate holding a bacon, egg, and cheese biscuit from McDonald's that a college student placed in the offering plate with love. On it was a little note that read, "You looked hungry. Silver and gold have I none; but such as I have give I thee."

What college students do bring is an abundance of questions. *Why should I believe that? Who says?* They aren't usually satisfied with "just because" answers, so I spend a lot of time discussing answers to those questions, but I always direct them back to the central question of faith: *Is Jesus really who he claimed to be?* We can endlessly debate which approaches to morality, life, politics, and science work best. But when we get down to the bedrock of our faith, the question is simply whether Jesus is who he said he was.

He claimed to be the very Voice of God. If he isn't, then we are free to pick and choose from his teachings like we would any other teacher. But if he is who he claimed to be, that changes the *way* that we ask our questions.

To illustrate this, I often use an analogy inspired by Plato, the ancient Greek philosopher:[1]

Suppose a group of people found themselves in a room with no windows, entrances, or exits. No one had ever gone out of the room, and no one had ever come in from outside. As far as they knew, they were the only people who had ever existed.

One day, the more philosophical among them begin to argue about what exists outside their room. One person believes it is a room identical to the one they are in. Another thinks it to be a room exactly opposite their room—a room where everything is backward. Another says that outside the room are hordes of roaming billy goats and mounds of feta cheese. Arguments back and forth get heated, with each one explaining why his or her theory is the most likely explanation.

What is ridiculous about their arguments, other than the billy goats and feta cheese? *They are arguing about realities beyond the realm of their knowledge.*

Their situation is not unlike the situation we're in when we try to figure out God, our origins, or our ultimate destiny. Even the most enlightened thinkers can only guess about the nature of God, how time began, or where everything is ultimately headed. No one was present for creation. No one understands even a fraction of our universe's complexities. No one has jumped ahead to see the finale of history. The more we learn about ourselves and our past, the more we realize we don't know.

Back to our room.

Suppose a being descended straight through the ceiling and hovered about six feet above the floor, telling everyone that he is *from* the other side of the wall. He tells us he created the room in which we are standing as well as each one of us, and he knows what our future holds.

Can the people in the room challenge the claims of this being? In one sense, *no*, since to challenge him they would need facts and experiences of their own. Do they have to accept his testimony? Again, *no*. They might conclude that this is some kind of illusion, a trick played by their fellow room-dwellers. They might conclude that the visitor is lying. They may even reject his words without a concrete reason. But if they choose to reject the being's claims, it is not because they can prove his claims are false. It is because they deny his claims to authority.

So what does this have to do with our faith? *Jesus showed up claiming to be the "being" from the other side of the wall.* He walked around claiming to be the Voice of God. He said things like, "If you've heard me, you've heard the Father" and "I descended from heaven to tell you the truth" and "I and my Father are one."[2] He assumed for himself every prerogative that belonged to God: he forgave sins, received worship, demanded absolute allegiance, commanded the weather, claimed to exist eternally and everywhere at once, and issued new Scripture on his own authority.[3] In no uncertain terms, he claimed to be God.

THE UNEXPLAINABLE MEETS THE UNDENIABLE

So, the question for us is *Is he who he said he was?* Did he give us any reason to believe he was the Voice of the I AM, the burning bush of the New Testament?

Jesus showed us in multiple ways that he was not an impostor. Scores of books have been written explaining these ways.[4] I will highlight only two.

Fulfilled Prophecy

Jesus's fulfillment of Old Testament prophecies is nothing short of breathtaking. In at least 322 places, Jewish prophets, who wrote hundreds of years before Jesus's birth, predicted details about the coming Messiah's life: he would be born in Bethlehem, from the tribe of Judah and the lineage of David, flee to Egypt as a kid, begin his ministry in Galilee, perform many miracles, enter as King into Jerusalem on a borrowed donkey, be betrayed by a friend for thirty pieces of silver, die by crucifixion between thieves, and then be resurrected and ascend to heaven—just to name a few.[5]

I've heard that when a foreign spy wants to appeal for asylum in the United States, the CIA gives him or her several layers of instruction to verify their identity so that there is no chance for a mistake. For example, one Soviet agent was told:

> Go to Mexico City. When there, (1) write a letter to the secretary of the US embassy requesting a meeting, signing your name as "I. Jackson." After three days (2) go to the Plaza de Colon in Mexico City and (3) stand before the statue of Columbus, (4) placing your middle finger in a guidebook. When approached, (5) say, "That is a magnificent statue," and (6) that you are only visiting from Oklahoma.[6]

If someone did all those things in the right sequence, the CIA could reasonably assume they had the right person and not someone who just showed up in the right place at the wrong time. God sent Jesus with more than *three hundred* such verifications.

Mathematicians say that the odds of those prophecies randomly coalescing on any one person is 1 in 10^{157}. (That's 10 with 157 zeroes after it. I wanted to put all the zeroes in here, but my publisher threatened to charge me personally for the extra ink. Trust me, it looks impressive.) To put that in perspective, 1 in 10^{16} would be the statistical probability of covering the entire surface area of North Carolina, South Carolina, and Georgia with silver dollars two feet deep, painting one red, and giving a blindfolded man one chance to pick the red one. Mathematicians conclude—in a principle called Borel's Law—that any odds beyond 1 in 10^{50} realistically have a zero probability of ever happening.[7] Jesus's fulfillment of prophecy is a strong indicator that he is who he said he was.

The Resurrection

A second thing that convinces me Jesus was not an impostor is the evidence for his resurrection from the dead. Looked at objectively, on the surface, the case for Jesus's resurrection is among the most-compellingly documented events in history. Nothing else can explain the birth of the Christian movement other than that the disciples were genuinely convinced that Jesus had risen.

The famed atheist-agnostic novelist Anne Rice was convinced there had to be a better explanation, and she set out to discover it. As an author, she had become known for her obsession with the underworld, her best-known books being *Interview with the Vampire* and *Memnoch the Devil*. What made her writing style unique was her wedding of that genre with careful attention to historical detail. She meticulously researched whatever era her stories were set in and then wove her fantastic tale through those details.[8]

When she was in her seventies, Rice began to research what she considered history's greatest mystery: what actually happened during the first century that gave rise to the "myth" of Jesus. Her plan was to retell the story with her characteristic insight into the darkness and superstitious bent of human nature.

Here's how she described her approach to her research:

> Having started with the skeptical critics ... I expected to discover that their arguments would be frighteningly strong, and that Christianity was, at heart, a kind of fraud. . . . Surely he [Jesus] was a liberal, married, had children, was a homosexual, and who knew what? But I must do my research before I wrote one word.

Her research revealed far more than she expected, however. After three years of meticulous study, she admitted,

> I was unconvinced by the wild postulations of those who claimed to be children of the Enlightenment. And I had also sensed something else. Many of these scholars, scholars who apparently devoted their life to New Testament scholarship, disliked Jesus Christ.
>
> In sum, the whole case for the nondivine Jesus who stumbled into Jerusalem and somehow got crucified by nobody and had nothing to do with the founding of Christianity and would be horrified by it if he knew about it—that whole picture which had floated in the liberal circles I frequented as an atheist for thirty years—that case was not made. Not only was it not made, I discovered in this field some of the worst and most biased scholarship I'd ever read.
>
> Christianity achieved what it did ... because Jesus rose from the dead. It was the fact of the resurrection that sent the apostles out into the world with the force necessary to create Christianity. Nothing else would have done it but that.[9]

Anne Rice is but one among many who have made the same discovery. The evidence really is overwhelming. I have to agree with Rice—only a preconceived bias against the *implications* of the resurrection could keep one from concluding that it actually happened.

What keeps most people from considering the story on its own terms is *what else* must be true if Jesus rose from the dead—namely, all that Jesus said about morality, his sovereign rule over the world, and his expressed purposes for history. Objection to the evidence is usually rooted in a dislike of his authority.

All this to say, Jesus did indeed give compelling reasons to believe that he was the "being" from the other side of the wall—not just an enlightened religious guru but the very presence of God come down to earth. His fulfillment of prophecy, his miracles, and his resurrection from the dead—not to mention the beauty of his life and the teaching itself—proved to me that he was telling the truth. I recognized in him the Voice of my Creator (John 10:27). Discovering him felt like walking out of a dark room into a well-lit one. When that happens, it's not logic that proves I am no longer in darkness. I know it because of what I can see. When God opens our hearts to hear Jesus, we just know he is the Voice of God (2 Cor 3:18–4:4).[10]

Perhaps you say, "Well, OK, Jesus seems trustworthy, but why trust the Bible? Isn't it just a book written by fallible, biased men?" Good question. Jesus promised the apostles that his Spirit would guide them in the accurate recording of his Word for future generations. He also promised that all authority in heaven and earth would be given to him for the completion of their mission to spread his message of salvation to the ends of the earth (Matt 16:18; 28:18; John 14:26; 17:20; 2 Tim 3:16–17). That certainly includes an accurate sending of his message. If I trust his claim to be the Messiah, I can also trust the Bible he left behind.

TAKING THE GIANT STEP OF FAITH

Once, when discussing the nature of salvation with a skeptical intellectual named Nicodemus, Jesus made a claim the skeptic thought was ridiculous—that people need to be "born again" before they can enter the kingdom of God. Nicodemus challenged, "*Why* would that be true, and *how* could it happen?" Jesus responded by basically saying, "Nicodemus, are you really in a position to question the logic of my assertions? Have you ascended into heaven and come back in a way that you would be able to verify these things? No one has ascended beyond the earth to figure these things out; rather, one has come down from heaven to *reveal* them" (John 3:1–14, my paraphrase).

In other words, we have neither the mental capacity nor the life experience to evaluate Jesus's claims about eternity. The question is: Is he who he says he is? We are presented with the same question posed to Moses: *Do you really believe that the* I AM *has spoken?*

If our faith depends on figuring out all the answers, we'll never possess *faith*. You see, faith is not a response to a convincing explanation but a convincing act of *revelation*. Faith happens when the unexplainable encounters the undeniable.[11] "Without faith," the writer of Hebrews says, "it is impossible to please God" (Heb 11:6). If you are going to know God, it will be because you believe he is who he says he is and trust him with things you cannot verify.

Let me share an example of what that kind of faith looks like.

During my senior year of college, I became good friends with a Muslim girl named Aisha who had grown up in Central Asia. She was spooky smart. I asked her if she would like to read the Bible with some friends of mine and me, and—more out of curiosity than anything else—she agreed to do so.

Somewhere along the way she became fascinated by Jesus. She bristled, however, at his claims to be God. As a Muslim, she had been drilled from birth with the idea that there can be no Trinity. I tried every analogy in the book to explain how God could be one being in three persons, but she kept saying, "I just can't see it."

One night I finally asked her, "Aisha, what if Jesus were to appear to you right here, right now, and say to you, 'I won't explain to you how this all works, but I want you to know that my claim to be God is true, and I want you to believe it and follow me even if you can't understand. Later I'll expand your thinking so it makes sense. But until then, I just need you to trust me.' Would you believe him?"

Aisha thought about the question for a moment and then told me that she wanted to go home and think about it some more.

The next morning, she called me at 7:00 a.m. She told me that during the middle of the night she had a dream that Jesus was knocking at her door. She got up to answer, and when she did, she realized she really did believe that Jesus is who he said he was. It was only fear, she admitted, keeping her from embracing it. But she knew that if he really was who he said he was, she could trust what he said to be true. That morning we prayed together, and she put her trust in Christ as Savior.

Your questions may not be about the Trinity. Maybe they are about why God would let a tsunami take the lives of 100,000 people in Southeast Asia. Or why your father got Alzheimer's disease. Or why God still hasn't brought along that special person for you to marry. Or why your spouse left. Or why God says certain kinds of sex, which feel so natural to you, are wrong. Or why so many people in the world aren't Christians if Christianity is actually true.

I've had many of these same questions. They are legitimate ones. But let me give it to you straight: God will not answer all those questions before he calls you to follow him. He didn't for Moses or the prophets or his disciples. He simply speaks—in an undeniable way, through burning bushes and empty tombs—and invites you to believe. If understanding everything is a prerequisite to belief, you'll never believe.

Each one of us must decide if we believe God is the Voice speaking. I always tell our college students that faith is accepting what you cannot understand on the basis of what you *can* understand. There are many things we may not be able to understand. What we can understand is that Jesus really is the Son of God. He proved that.

That doesn't mean all our questions will vanish the moment we believe. They didn't for Jesus's disciples:

When many of his disciples heard [these things], they said, "This is a hard saying: who can listen to it?" . . . After this many of his disciples turned back and no longer walked with him. So Jesus said to the twelve, "Do you want to go away as well?" Simon Peter answered him, "Lord, to whom shall we go? You have the words of eternal life, and we have believed, and have come to know, that you are the Holy One of God." (John 6:60, 66–69 ESV)

I love Peter's answer. It's authentic, even if a little uninspiring: "Leave? Uhhh . . . where else can we go? Your words confuse us and sometimes anger us, but they are the only ones that give life."

Having faith does not mean having all your questions answered but perceiving that there is One who does have all the answers. Like Peter, your faith may be filled with questions. There will undoubtedly be moments where you have nothing else but Peter's confession: "We have believed, and have come to know, that you are the Holy One of God."

What we must avoid at all costs is editing Jesus, forcing him into a mold where he answers our questions the way we like. This is not worship of God; it's worship of ourselves. And it is the greatest substitute for true faith.

CHAPTER 7

YOU DON'T GET YOUR OWN PERSONAL JESUS

When I arrived at the boarding gate, only two other people were waiting to board the late-night flight from Ft. Lauderdale, Florida, to Charlotte, North Carolina. One was a gentleman I estimated to be two hundred years old. The other was a mysterious, brooding young woman in her early twenties with deep brown eyes. I was young and single, so I prayed about where to sit and felt "clearly led" to sit next to the girl.

She was from Chile, and her name was Berta. She had a strong accent and rolled her r's whenever she said her name, so it came out *Berrrrrrrrta*. She was returning to Boston, Massachusetts, where she lived on campus at Harvard University. I'd just graduated from Campbell University—"the Harvard of the South"—so immediately I felt we had a bond.

Conversation turned toward what we were doing with our lives, and I told her God had called me into ministry. I explained how I had come to faith in Christ, how he had changed my life, and how I now wanted to spend the rest of my life telling other people about him.

The whole time I talked, she stared at me with those deep, brooding eyes. She said, "You know, at Harvard I am around some of the most driven, intelligent men in the world. But I don't think I've ever heard anyone speak about life with such conviction and purpose."

I thought, "This is awesome! I'm going to lead this girl to Christ, and then we're going to get married. This will make a great story for the times I introduce her at Christian conferences and book signings."

We talked about Jesus for nearly the entire flight. As we began our descent into Charlotte, I thought I better close the deal (um, for Jesus). So I said, "Berrrrta, would you like to trust Jesus as *your* Savior?"

Without giving it much thought, she said, "No . . . you know, that kind of stuff has just never worked for me. I am so happy that you have found your peace in Jesus, but I relate to my God in a different way."

"But Berrrrta," I said. "Jesus said in John 14:6 that he was the only way to come to God. He provided a salvation for us that we could not provide for ourselves. He's not just my way, Berta; he's the only way."

She said, "Surely you are not saying that your way is the only way to God."

I said, "Berrrta, I don't think you understand. It's not my way, it's *his* way. And *I* am not saying that; *Jesus* said that."

"You're trying to tell me that if I don't accept Jesus the way that you have, I won't go to heaven?"

"Well, yes."

"That has to be the most arrogant, closed-minded thing I've ever heard someone say. I can't believe anyone today would be so bigoted as to think that there is only one way to God. What kind of God is that? That's not a God I want to know."

At that point, I suspected the wedding was off.

I sat there in my seat, a little shell-shocked, unsure of what to say next. As the pilot announced our final descent into Charlotte, I said: "Berrrrta, I sure am glad the pilot of this airplane doesn't look at the airport the way you look at truth."[1]

"What do you mean?"

"Say he announces, 'You know, I am sick of that arrogant little "control tower" always saying I've got to land this 737 on a narrow little strip of cement they call a "runway." That's their way, not mine. I am an open-minded pilot, so today I am going to land on the interstate. Or try to balance this aircraft nose first on the tip of the Bank of America building downtown.' Personally, I'm glad that our pilot chooses to enter the airport along that narrow little way the control tower lays out for him."

She said, "That's not a fair comparison."

I said, "Yes, it is. And that's Campbell University, 1; Harvard, 0, if you're keeping score."

I probably should have been more gracious. But even amidst my wounded ego and the crushed dreams of a Chilean wedding, I stand by that comparison.

YOUR OWN PERSONAL JESUS?

Like Berta, very few people object when I say that Jesus Christ is *my* Savior. Some even find it "attractive." It's when I go on to say the rest of what Jesus says—that he is the only way to God and the authority on all matters in life and death—that they cry foul. Our culture's problem is not with Jesus as a good man, a prophet, a teacher, or even as a deity. It's with Jesus's primary claim, that he is Lord.

Sometimes I hear people talk about "my God" or "my Jesus" as if he were their possession. Once, I was listening to two people on a talk show debate the Christian perspective on some moral issue. One, to her credit, was trying to explain what the Bible said. The other, who was a bit more "free-thinking," kept saying indignantly, "Well, *my* Jesus would never say that." The individual referred to "his Jesus" so many times that I finally yelled at the television, "You don't get your own personal Jesus!" I'm aware that he couldn't hear me. But it still felt right at the time.

God is not "ours." He is his own. He's not a salad bar where we take the items we have an appetite for and leave the others. He's not the Burger King God, where you "have him your way," or a Build-A-Bear God, where you assemble the deity you like best.

When God appeared to Moses, he declared, "I am who I am." "I am who I am" is not "I am whoever you want me to be."

Can we imagine how offensive it must be to God when we attempt to reshape him according to our preferences? How would you like it if someone did that to you? Suppose a writer approached you and said, "I have been watching you, and I'd really like to write your biography. I want other people to know how wonderful you are." But then their biography presents you as an astronaut with a string of failed relationships who lives alone with eighteen cats, none of which are true. So, you say to your biographer, "Uhhh . . . there's a problem. First, I'm scared of heights; second, I am not *that* bad at relationships; and third, like all godly people, I prefer dogs to cats."

They respond, "Oh, but you are so much more interesting as the spurned, cat-loving astronaut. People will only buy the book if you're like that."[2]

My guess is that you'd be offended. If we wouldn't like someone else doing that to us, why would we think it's OK to do that with God? Do we think that our idea of God is better than who he actually is?

Have we forgotten who we are talking about?

REMAKING GOD IN OUR IMAGE

When it comes to creating a God of our liking, a quip attributed to Voltaire holds true: "God created man in His own image, and man has been trying to repay the favor ever since." God recognized this would be one of our greatest temptations, so in the second commandment he warned, "You shall not make for yourself an image in the form of anything in heaven above or on the earth beneath or in the waters below" (Exod 20:4).

We must be careful not to confuse this commandment with the first one, "You shall have no other gods before me," as people often do. They might sound similar, but they are different. The first is about worshiping the *wrong* gods. The second is about worshiping the right God *in the wrong way.*

If you want to know how much of a temptation this is for us, consider that Israel broke this commandment before Moses had even come back down the mountain with the commandments.

Moses had been delayed in his return, and the people got scared. The promises of an invisible God were not enough for them, not when there were real needs, real enemies, and real dangers. They wanted a protector they could touch and see, whose presence they could verify. So they made a golden calf to represent God.

Notice how the narrator makes clear that with the golden calf Israel was not worshiping a *new* god but the true God in the wrong way: "When Aaron saw this, he built an altar in front of the calf and announced, 'Tomorrow there will be a festival to the LORD'" (Exod 32:5–6). "LORD" in all caps indicates God's *covenant* name given specially to Israel. For the Israelites, this golden image became the one true God "as-we-would-like-him-to-be."

We might be tempted to think that no one does this anymore. You probably don't have a golden calf in your basement. And you probably haven't melted down your wedding ring into an amulet you pray to. However, we make "graven images" whenever we edit God into a shape we'd prefer.

Sometimes, for example, we elevate one attribute of God above all the others. Maybe we prefer a God of love who is lax on judgment, accepting of all lifestyles, and open to all sincere attempts at self-salvation. Or maybe we like to think of God as hating whomever we hate. Or maybe we prefer a God who guarantees financial prosperity and promises to keep us from all pain.

Thomas Jefferson, one of the Founding Fathers of the United States, loved many of the teachings of Jesus but found his miracles to be backward and distasteful. He wanted to be able to read the parts of the Bible he liked without being troubled by the parts he didn't, so he literally cut them out. On display in the Smithsonian Museum is Jefferson's Bible with various stories and teachings by Jesus removed.

I don't approve of Jefferson's approach, but I admire his honesty. We may not have physically cut out parts of the Bible, but do we follow Jefferson's approach in our beliefs?

The pivotal question of faith is whether we are willing to accept God as he presents himself. Do we approach God listening for his "*I am*," or do we quickly declare to him, "*You should be . . .*"?

One way we can tell if we've "remade" God in our image is by how often our "God" contradicts and offends us. If our God only affirms what we already think, we're probably not listening to him and instead deifying our own convictions. After all, any independent person has their own ideas and opinions which unavoidably conflict with ours. How much more should we expect this with God?

A new reality show called *90 Day Fiancé* recently caught my attention. Volunteers fill out a questionnaire that helps them describe their ideal spouse. Based on their answers, producers match them up with someone. Then they put them, sight unseen, together in a house for ninety days.

You can imagine what happens. At first it seems like everything is perfect; their match seems perfectly tailored to their liking. Inevitably, however, one partner does something the other doesn't expect. A difference of opinion is revealed and conflict ensues. The newly coupled pair then has to choose: Do I like the actual person or only my version of this person?

Even though my wife and I *chose* each other after many months of friendship and dating, she still does things now that surprise and confuse me. Often her opinions conflict with mine. That's part of being in relationship with an independent person. If that's what living with another *human* is like, how much more should we expect that with *God*? Especially when we consider how much greater and wiser than us he is and how sinful and twisted our hearts actually are (Jer 17:9), should we really expect him to agree with us most of the time?

As theologian Karl Barth said, "If God doesn't make us mad, we're not worshiping him, but ourselves."[3] If our "God" never contradicts us and always likes what we like and hates what we hate, he's not the real God. All we've done is deified our preferences and called the personification of those things "God."

SPIRITUAL DEFORMITY

The irony is that when we reshape God into our image, the result is not the bolder, more confident faith we imagined, but spiritual deformity. God designed the human heart to be complete and free in *himself*—that is, the *true* version of himself. As appealing as rival conceptions of him may appear on the surface, they never quite fit. They're not God enough.

Exodus 32 tells us that as soon as the people made this golden image, moral mayhem broke out. "They celebrated with feasting and drinking, and they indulged in pagan revelry" (Exod 32:6 NLT). "Pagan revelry" means "open orgy."

In the same way, our reshaped God feels liberating at first. But inevitably, we become like what we worship. If our conception of God comes out of our hearts, which are by nature spiritually dark (Jer 17:9), rather than illuminate our darkness, our "God" makes it worse.

Some ancient tribal cultures loved violence, for example, so they fashioned gods who gloried in conquest. As a result, they became increasingly cruel and violent. Jews of Jesus's day were proud of their Jewish heritage, and so they saw God in increasingly nationalistic ways. Those of us who have grown up in a consumeristic Western culture envision an Americanized Jesus who is one part genie, one part fan club, one part financial advisor, one part American patriot, and several parts therapist. Our "God" makes us more narcissistic and materialistic, not less.

Those in progressive, liberal cultures often prefer to think of Jesus as a morally permissive deity wearing Birkenstocks who functions like a big cosmic blanket in which they can curl up and find themselves. In doing so, they become more and more licentious and self-absorbed, not less.

Problems in our behavior always trace back to corruption in our worship. Saint Augustine called stress, worry, anxiety, strife, jealousy, and dissatisfaction smoke rising from the altars we've erected to our false gods. Trace the trail of this smoke back to its source, and you'll likely find a distorted or incomplete view of God. For example,

- If you tend to be harsh and judgmental toward others, you have not experienced God as gracious.
- If you find yourself rarely in conflict with society around you, your God is not transcendent.
- If you worry a lot, your God is not the good, wise, and sovereign God of the Bible.
- If you can't shake the feeling that you are condemned, your God is not a faithful, redeeming Father.
- If you argue all the time about theology but never tell anyone about Jesus, your God is not a savior but only a professor.
- If you find yourself constantly jealous of what other people have, your God is not glorious and all-sufficient.

Like the children of Israel, we go searching for a God to better suit our felt needs but end up drowning in a sea of fear, despair, and moral chaos. Our reshaped gods, whom we hoped would bring us

security and comfort, are utterly incapable to give us the love, fulfillment, and assurance for which we yearn.

God created us for *himself*—gods of our own making will never
do the job. They are not God enough. Like the children of Israel,
we have to choose which god to pursue: an infinite God who will
sometimes confuse us and contradict us, or a small god that neither
satisfies nor saves us.

WHO IS CARRYING WHOM?

Maybe the most pathetic part of Israel creating their own "God"
is that they now had the burden of caring for this "God." He didn't
comfort them; they had to dance for him. He couldn't even move
himself from place to place; they had to carry him!

What a terrible trade! The true God had promised to supply all
their needs, protect them when they were afraid, satisfy them when
they were thirsty, and feed them when they were hungry. He promised never to leave them. One day, he would give his life to redeem
them. They traded this God for an image of an animal assembled
from leftover earrings and bracelets.

You can take one of two postures toward God. You can shrink
him down and carry him, or humble yourself and let him carry you.
If you attempt to carry him, you will retain a measure of control, but
he won't satisfy you. If he carries you, you must relinquish all control
and be ready to *receive* all he says whether it sits well with you or not.

A few years ago, I was sitting in a crowded airport waiting
area. Our flight had been delayed *again*, and I was trying to get
some reading done. (Does Delta stand for "Doesn't Ever Leave the
Airport"?) I looked up to see the eyes of a friendly, older lady fixed
firmly on mine. She asked me what I was reading, and I told her it
was a Christian book about discovering God's love. Her eyes lit up,
and she said that she too was a spiritual seeker. She ran a shop on a
beach in Florida where she sold religious amulets.

"All religions teach good things," she said, "And I collect the best from each one. I find something good in them all, and I try to share the best parts with others."

We talked for several minutes about what she thought those things were, and I shared with her my faith in Christ.

"Oh yes," she responded. "Christianity teaches many good things." At that point, she reached inside her bag and pulled out a small rosary ring with a crucifix attached to it. "This is what I've taken from the Catholics. It reminds me of God's power, and I always carry it when I travel, because it keeps me safe."

I was trying to figure out how to respond to that when an elderly lady sitting across from us turned to her husband with her newspaper in hand and said in a voice loud enough for the dead to hear, "Honey, our horoscope predicts that our travels will be safe today!"

The woman I was talking to immediately turned and said, "Really? That's great news! My friend here (she pointed to me) is a Christian pastor, so he'll bring us good luck as we fly too." And then, out of nowhere, another guy—a guy I *thought* had been busy with his Sudoku puzzle—leaned forward and said, "I have St. Christopher right here in my bag."

I looked at him and thought, "What bag? Can St. Christopher really ride along as a carry-on?"

Sure enough, he reached into his duffle bag and pulled out a foot-high statue of St. Christopher, the patron saint of traveling. The lady I was talking to smiled from ear to ear: "We are sure to have safe travels now—a positive horoscope, my rosary ring, St. Christopher, and a Baptist pastor!"

Seminary did not prepare me for this. The gate attendant summoned us to begin boarding. As we walked down the jetway together, she handed me the rosary ring and very kindly said, "I want you to have this rosary ring. Remember, if you'll hold onto it when we take off and land, it will keep you safe."

As she placed it in my hand, I couldn't help but noticing the image of Jesus hanging on the cross engraved on the top. This is the God who promises to hold us in his hand if we'll submit to him (John 10:29). I am in his hand when I take off, and I'll be in his hand when I land. And if we happen to explode midflight, I'll still remain in his hand.

If he holds me in his hand, you see, I don't have to be as concerned about clinging so tightly to him with mine.

Our hearts yearn for the security and satisfaction that comes from knowing the all-sufficient, eternally wise, and all-powerful God. But the only way we can know him is to come to him on his terms—to receive him for who he is. And that means being willing to hear from him things that sometimes confuse you. As Tim Keller says, only the faith that believes God regarding things it doesn't want to hear can believe God about the things it desperately *does* want to hear.[4]

We each have to decide if we want a fake god—an imaginary god we can carry around—or the real God, who is beyond our understanding and control, who carries us.

If you are searching for bold, world-transforming faith, a god of your own making simply will not do. Only by humbling yourself before God and receiving him on his terms will you encounter the God worth living for and a faith worth dying for.

The God behind all of creation is the God that you crave—a God large enough to satisfy your deepest desires and wise enough to rule our universe. He is a God whose love, glory, and majesty you've always yearned for, even if you didn't know how to express it. And he is unwaveringly good, even if we can't always understand what he is doing.

PART 2

GOD IS GOOD

If there is one [subject] which . . . makes me go back from this platform utterly ashamed of my poor feeble words, it is this subject. This love of Christ is the most amazing thing under heaven, if not in heaven itself.

CHARLES SPURGEON[1]

CHAPTER 8

THE GOD WE CRAVE

I'm missing something."

That's the shared sentiment of almost every person who has ever walked the face of the earth. Strangely enough, it ties in to why we don't like to be naked in public.

According to Genesis, the first thing Adam and Eve felt after they had sinned against God was that something was missing—namely, their clothes: "Then the eyes of both of them were opened, and they realized they were naked; so they sewed fig leaves together and made coverings for themselves" (Gen 3:7).

The truth is, they had been naked since creation, but only after sinning did it bother them. What changed? Saint Augustine had a great answer: prior to their sin, Adam and Eve felt "clothed" in the love and acceptance of God.[1] Having been stripped of that, they felt exposed. Something wasn't right. Something was missing. They went from perfect security to "naked and afraid."

How did they react? The way normal people who find themselves naked in public have reacted ever since. If you have a problem sleepwalking and suddenly wake to find yourself standing in a Super Walmart stark naked, your first instinct is probably not to pick up a few odds-and-ends for the house. You run to the clothing section to put something on and pray no one who knows you sees you. This is not a time for multitasking.

Adam and Eve's response to their nakedness typifies how we now go through life. Our souls *feel* naked. Life therefore becomes a quest to find that "thing"—that relationship, that possession, that achievement—that will make us feel accepted, significant, secure, loved—"clothed" again. We turn to the "fig leaves" of family, romance, power, approval, comfort, or control. But try as we may, these clothes never quite seem to fit. That's because what we're missing is much, much greater than anything the earth can supply. We are missing the love and acceptance of the Almighty God.

Eighteenth-century French philosopher Blaise Pascal explained it this way: "There was once in man a true happiness, of which all that now remains is the empty print and trace. . . . This infinite abyss can be filled only with an infinite and immutable object; in other words, by God himself."[2]

Each of us is born with a humongous, God-sized vacuum in our heart. All the things we try to replace God with—family, success, sex, friendships, travel, fame, drugs, pornography—leave us empty. They may make us feel, for a while, like we're closing in on happiness. But, inevitably, they leave us yearning for more. They just aren't big enough—not God enough—to satisfy us.

DRY WELLS

Artist-musician Madonna made a career out of pushing the limits of morality. Every few years she seemed to come out with something more outrageous. Tim Keller references a statement she made in an interview with *Vogue* magazine where she explained why:

> My drive in life comes from a fear of being mediocre. That is always pushing me. I push past one spell of it and discover myself as a special human being but then I feel I am still mediocre and

uninteresting unless I do something else. Because even though I have become somebody, I still have to prove that I am somebody. My struggle has never ended and I guess it never will.[3]

In other words, she recognized that her abnormal behavior came from a place of emptiness. Even after all her success, she still felt naked. She continued to search for something that would make her feel special and significant.

The prophet Jeremiah diagnosed her craving nearly three thousand years ago, when he described the twofold dimension of soul-emptiness: "My people have committed two evils: they have forsaken me, the fountain of living waters, and hewed out cisterns for themselves, broken cisterns that can hold no water" (Jer 2:13). We rejected God, who was to us like a fresh, ever-flowing fountain of joy, and in his absence we turned to "broken cisterns," which couldn't hold the "living water" we needed. Cisterns, in those days, were small pits lined with rock, designed to collect rainwater. But they usually leaked, so any water you collected eventually seeped out. Jesus picked up on Jeremiah's analogy and illustrated it in the life of a broken woman he met in a very unlikely place.

FIVE BROKEN CISTERNS

Jesus sat down one afternoon at a well in a Samarian city and asked a woman, who was the only other person there at the time, if she would get him something to drink. Jews normally didn't mingle with Samaritans, and she demurred because the two ethnicities had a long-standing hatred of each other. Jesus ignored her rebuff and responded, "If you knew the gift of God, and who it is that is saying to you, 'Give me a drink,' you would have asked him, and he would have given you living water" (John 4:10 ESV).

The Greek phrase for "living water" literally means "flowing water," the kind of water that runs in deep, pure, underground rivers. It's cold and clear—unlike the tepid, stagnant water she was pulling out of the city well. She didn't yet realize he was being spiritual. She was legitimately curious. *What well is he talking about?*

Sensing her confusion, Jesus said, *I'm talking about a different kind of water*: "Everyone who drinks of this water will be thirsty again, but whoever drinks of the water that I will give him will never be thirsty again" (4:13–14 ESV).

If she was in a mist before, now she's in a fog. Drink one time from a well and never be thirsty again? She probably assumed he was mocking her, and she responded scornfully: "Sir, give me this water so that I won't get thirsty and have to keep coming here to draw water" (4:15).

She's attempting to call his bluff.

Oddly, however, Jesus responds by telling her to go get her husband.

She stutters, "But . . . I don't have a husband." And even if she did, what would he have to do with anything?

Jesus responds, "That's right. You have no husband now. But you've had five husbands, and the guy you are sleeping with now is not your husband."

If you were writing the musical score for this scene, this is where you'd cue the dramatic "gotcha" music.

She's been exposed. What was more was that adultery in those days was a capital offense. What Jesus knew about her could get her killed.

Yet Jesus was not trying to startle, embarrass, or threaten her. He was trying to show her what he meant by living water. This woman had been doing the same thing with her lovers that she was doing with the city well. No matter how much she drank each day, she always woke up the next day thirsty.

Blessings like marriage, family, sex, money, and popularity are wonderful, but if you try to put them in the place of God, they will leave you thirsty. Attempting to replace God in your heart is what the Bible calls "idolatry." It's when you take a good thing—like marriage or money—and turn it into a "god" thing. Then it inevitably becomes a disappointing thing.

That's precisely what the woman had been doing at the well of romance. When she met that first man who would become her husband, she probably thought, "This is it! This is what I've always dreamed of—to be special to someone." And maybe she was happy for a while. But then something went wrong—maybe it was his fault, or maybe hers. Either way, she ended up alone.

Along came man number two. This time she thought, "Well, I'm wiser now. I won't make the mistakes I made last time." Marriage number two began. It fell apart too.

Rinse and repeat the process with husbands three, four, and five. By the time Jesus met her, she'd apparently given up on the idea of marriage altogether. She assumed that "free love" was the path to a happy life. But there she stood, still thirsty. And ashamed. And asking the same question millions of us ask ourselves every day: What's *missing*?

Had she just not met the right man?

No. She was drinking from the wrong well.

People approach romance like a drowning man approaches a life preserver. He's drowning in a sea of loneliness and despair when along floats a five-foot-two blonde life preserver, so he lunges for it.

The life raft of romance, however, was not designed to bear the weight of our souls, and by clutching it so tightly we threaten to drown both our lover and ourselves. Lonely, insecure single people become lonely, insecure married people. If anything, they become worse. That's because problems like loneliness and insecurity cannot be cured by the love of another human being.

Ernest Becker, an agnostic anthropologist and winner of the Pulitzer Prize, observed,

> Modern society, after having ceased to believe in God . . . turned
> to the romantic partner as a replacement. The self-glorification

that we need in our innermost being, we now look for in the love partner. The love partner becomes the divine ideal within which to fulfill one's life.[4]

Becker then noted that we can hear this illustrated in today's popular love songs. Most love songs sound quasi religious, as if romance is a spiritual pursuit. Jordin Sparks sings, "Losing you is like living in a world with no air." Bruno Mars laments that losing his latest girlfriend felt like losing "the sun" from his life. Hozier tells his girlfriend that she is heaven's "true mouthpiece" and that being with her is like "going to church."

Romantic love, when it becomes our most important thing, disappoints. Hip-hop star Drake admitted,

> There was a point where I felt like I needed to keep the company of a different woman every night. I was trying to fill a void. But in those moments after sex, I'd know it wasn't working. Those quiet moments are the realest moments a man will ever have in his life. . . . The next day I'd convince myself to do it again. But during that time, I knew it wasn't working.[5]

I often tell couples in premarital counseling that if they would let me, before their ceremony, I would write with a permanent marker on each of their foreheads, "Warning: Cannot support the weight of your soul," like one of those signs in front of an old mountain bridge warning that it cannot support gigantic loads. Your romantic partner is just not designed to sustain the weight of your soul. Only the love of God can.

King Solomon observed that God had created us with eternity in our hearts (Eccl 3:11). Your soul has an *eternal* thirst. Only an *eternal* God can fill it. Other gods will not work; they are not God enough.

Maybe romance is not your well of choice, but every person chooses a well from which to seek soul satisfaction. It's the essence of what it means to be a sinner (Rom 1:23).

What is it for you? When you imagine your future, what

absolutely needs to be there for you to feel happy? What are those things that, if you lost them, would make life not worth living?

Those things are your "well."

Maybe your well is career success. Maybe it is a stable, happy family. Or financial security. Maybe it's being known as the best at what you do—having your jersey suspended from the rafters, so to speak.

Like the well of romance, these things provide thrilling satisfaction—for a while. But then we wake up thirsty.

A CHOICE OF FOUR

Tim Keller says that when we experience the inevitable disappointment that comes from drinking out of a broken cistern, we respond in one of four ways:

Blame the idol. We assume that we simply chose the wrong idol and resolve to make a better choice next time. "Well, our marriage fell apart because she just wasn't the right person for me. We were so young when we got married and I didn't know what I needed in a partner. I know there is a soul mate out there for me somewhere. . . . I just haven't found her yet. Someone who will never disappoint or fail me, someone who will never cease to make me happy." Sure. She's right over there next to that unicorn and pot of gold. You keep drawing from the well.

Blame yourself. "I am the problem. There's something wrong with *me*." "I didn't work hard enough." "I'm always messing things up." So, you resolve to do better. Turn over a new leaf. Clean up your proverbial desk. Which lasts for about two days, and then you revert to the same sloppy jerk you always were. With every new failure, you get closer to despair.

Blame the world. You give up on finding happiness and become cynical, mocking all those naïve idealists who actually think happiness is out there. You grow bored with life and callous in relationships. You medicate through alcohol or drugs or materialism (i.e., retail therapy). Perhaps you plunge yourself into some isolating, engrossing hobby. Or you write alternative music and angry blogs and troll happy people on Twitter.

Realize that you were created for another world. Maybe the reason nothing in this world satisfies you is that it wasn't *designed* to satisfy you. The world is not God enough. If *God* is what we are missing, we won't find satisfaction in a soul mate, a salary, or a syringe. As C. S. Lewis said, "If I find in myself a desire which no experience in this world can satisfy, the most probable explanation is that I was made for another world."[6]

TOO WONDERFUL FOR ME

Deep in our souls, like the woman at the well, we thirst for joy, security, meaning, unconditional love, and belonging.

Our thirst for these things is not wrong. The places we seek them are.

The glory of God is the water for which we thirst. His love is the security that we seek. His presence is the clothing we feel desperate for. King David explained in Psalm 139 that God's love finally gave him what he was looking for:

> O LORD, you have searched me and known me! . . .
> For you formed my inward parts;
>   you knitted me together in my mother's womb.
> I praise you, for I am fearfully and wonderfully made.
> Wonderful are your works;
>   my soul knows it very well. . . .
> Your eyes saw my unformed substance;
> in your book were written, every one of them,
>   the days that were formed for me,
>   when as yet there was none of them. (Ps 139:1, 13–14, 16 ESV)

God saw me in the womb. Before my mom even knew she was pregnant, he knew everything there was to know about me. And he loved me. He carefully planned my life and chose every one of my days, sending his angels to watch over me in both the good times and the bad. Not even a single hair falls from my head without his knowledge (Matt 10:30).

When our kids were young, I was constantly amazed at how aware my wife, Veronica, was of even their smallest physical features. "J. D., did you see that Ryah has a new freckle behind her right ear?" And I would say, "Which one is Ryah, again?" Just kidding. Yet God knows me better and watches me more closely than the most attentive, love-stricken mother.

As Psalm 139:6–8 says,

> Such knowledge is too wonderful for me;
> it is high; I cannot attain it.
> Where shall I go from your Spirit?
> Or where shall I flee from your presence?
> If I ascend to heaven, you are there!
> If I make my bed in hell, you are there! (ESV)[7]

You literally *can't get away* from God's love! Even if you made your bed in *hell*, God wouldn't leave you there.

The truth is, we *did* make our bed in hell. We told God to leave us alone and ran as far away from him as we could. Yet he kept thinking about us. Even as we pounded nails into his hands and feet, he cried out, "Father, forgive them, for they know not what they do" (Luke 23:34 ESV). He wouldn't let go.

No wonder David says,

> How precious to me are your thoughts, God!
> How vast the sum of them!
> Were I to count them,
> they would outnumber the grains of sand—
> when I awake, I am still with you. (Ps 139:17–18)

You are *precious* to God (Isa 43:4). If one of my kids contracted a disease for which the only cure was an exorbitantly expensive medicine, without hesitation I would mortgage every earthly possession I had to get that medicine. That's because they are *precious* to me. The God who spoke the galaxies into existence, and could do it all over again if he wanted, finds you *precious*. He was willing to face humiliation, torture, and scorn just to buy you back.

Do you ache to be special to someone? You are.

Do you want to be known, valued, and approved of? You are.

God's love is richer, deeper, and lasts longer than any other love! You matter so much to God he literally *cannot stop thinking about you*, as King David says.

The arms you search for in romance are his arms. The fullness you yearn for is found in his presence. The security you seek is found in his promises.

He is the living water you thirst for.

LEAVING BEHIND RELIGION

Let's go back once more to Jesus and the woman at the well because she makes a mistake that many people make when they realize something is missing from their lives: *she gets religious*. After Jesus revealed the brokenness of her soul, she tried to turn the conversation into a religious debate: "Our ancestors worshiped on this mountain, but you Jews claim that the place where we must worship is in Jerusalem" (John 4:20).

In the same way, many people turn to religion to avoid the hard questions about God. What religion seeks is a small god who can be placated with ritual and plugged into the margins of our lives. That kind of god won't satisfy our souls.

Jesus explained to this woman that there is only one way to be happy: to worship God *in spirit and truth* (John 4:24 ESV). But what does that mean exactly? If God is seeking it, we should be clear on it.

In spirit

Knowing God in *spirit* means making him your primary life source. God does not merely want to be a part of your life; he wants to be the core of it. In that sense, God is not satisfied merely to be "number one" in our hearts, he wants to be the *only* one. Imagine a husband saying to his wife, "Sweetheart, I want you to know that you are the number one girl in my life. Julie, Sarah, and Amy are numbers two, three, and four, but you are number one!"

Romantic commitments require exclusivity. Worship commitments do too. You can only experience ultimate satisfaction, security, and peace from one place.

Several years ago, the popular Christian bumper sticker was "Jesus is my co-pilot." I always hated it. If Jesus is your co-pilot, somebody is in the wrong seat. Coming to Jesus means acknowledging that it's his car and you stole it. You hand him the keys, get in the back seat, and ask where he would like to go next.

Knowing Jesus requires a total, unconditional surrender of your spirit. He becomes your identity, your goal, and your hope.

In truth

Not only must God occupy the central place in your spirit, you can't hide anything from him. We have to get "soul-naked" before him. But like this woman, that presents a dilemma. How can we hope to be accepted by him if everything is exposed?

After Jesus exposed this woman in all her guilt and emptiness, he didn't walk away. That's because just a few months later he would go to a cross where he would take her death sentence upon himself. There he clothed her in his righteousness. Even as a sinner, she was safe in his presence and through him secure in the Father's love.

This story poses a question we all wonder subconsciously in our hearts: What is it like to be completely exposed in all your shame and guilt before God?

The answer?

It's safe. In fact, it's the only safe place in the universe.

Like this woman, we each carry around a sense of condemnation that separates us from the God we crave. We want to be loved unconditionally and known fully. To be loved without being known feels shallow, and to be known without being loved is rejection. And therein lies our dilemma. We feel too guilty to expose ourselves to the God we crave. Naked and ashamed, we hide. Naked and ashamed, we die.

The cross of Jesus is the answer to our dilemma. When we expose our souls to him, he receives us, forgives us, cleanses us, and saves us. We find in his eternal love the well for which our soul has been searching.

MAKING THE LEAP

To expose yourself like this to God takes faith. Scary faith. You have to believe that he really is the one for whom your soul is created and that he is gracious enough to receive you—even with all your sin and shame.

For years, I shared Christ with the mechanic who worked on my car. He was as country as they come and a genius with an engine. Whenever I brought him my car, we would talk about Jesus. After a few minutes he'd say, "I know, J. D. I know I need Jesus, but I also know that if you're really going to follow Jesus, you have to give it all to him, and I'm just not sure I can do that yet."

One afternoon, he pulled his cigarette out of his mouth and asked me to pray for him because the doctor had discovered a spot in his lungs. I did, and we talked for more than an hour about his need for Jesus. Still he struggled with releasing everything in his life.

I finally told him, "Jack, you are just going to have to let go. But I promise you it's safe. Jesus won't drop you."

He nodded his head, thanked me, and I got in the car to leave.

As I was backing out of his driveway, I saw him walking back toward my car, so I stopped and rolled down the window.

"Son, I've got to tell you a story," he said.

"The other day I was working back here on a car, and I heard the most awful moaning sound coming from that house over there. It sounded like a cow dying. When I went over to see what the problem was, I saw this seventeen-year-old kid hanging on to that chimney up there. He had climbed up on his roof to clean the gutters, but when he got up there, he panicked. I told him not to worry; I'd hold the ladder while he climbed down. To do that, of course, he'd have to let go of the chimney, which he wasn't going to do. So I climbed up the ladder and extended my hand to him. He said he was still too scared to let go of the chimney. I stood there arguing with him for about five minutes. Finally, I said, 'Son, if you don't grab my hand, I'm going to have to knock you off this chimney. Either way, you're coming down.'"

Then he said, "J. D., I think that's what God is doing to me. He's trying to knock me loose so I will hold on to him."

Pretty good theology, I told him. We baptized him next Easter.

It's a lot more pleasant when God doesn't have to "knock your grip loose," but he will if he has to. He's trying to get you to see that no other foundation can support you. No other presence can clothe you. No other water can satisfy you.

For many people, however, there's something significant that stands in the way of releasing themselves to him. While they may be attracted to the love of an eternal God, they resent the idea of a God who would judge them for their sin. If there is one thing that causes more people in the Western world to take offense with Jesus, it's God's anger about our sin.

What do you do when you realize the God you crave is also the God you sometimes hate?

CHAPTER 9

THE GOD WE HATE

A lot of people assume that because I am a pastor that I have it all together—at least spiritually. They assume that I roll over each morning, open my eyes, and sigh with contentment, "Good morning, Lord!" Then I grab the harp beside my bed and pluck out a few psalms I composed in my dreams. Spiritually refreshed and smiling, I go downstairs where all my kids sit around the table with their Bibles open. In unison they say, "Daddy, teach us God's Word before we start the day."

But that's not typically how my day starts. Usually I wake up to the sound of one kid complaining that his sister put her fingers in his milk. My first thought is not usually, "Good morning, Lord," but something more along the lines of, "Good Lord . . . is it already morning?" And after dinner when I say, "Hey kids, let's read the Bible," they say, "Not yet, Dad. Mom promised us thirty minutes of TV time."

So my life may look a lot more like yours than you think. The questions I ask about God and faith are probably not that different from yours, either. Like many, I've struggled with the concept of God's wrath. Many believe it's unfair. What was so bad about a bite from a forbidden fruit? Or what could we possibly do during our eighty years on earth that could warrant an *eternity* in hell?

Even the great C. S. Lewis admitted, "There is no doctrine which

I would more willingly remove from Christianity than this, if it lay in my power."[1] I've often felt the same way. Give me a divine eraser and an hour, and I'll give you a Bible without God's wrath.

But we can't remove God's wrath from the Bible. And I want to show you in this chapter that if we properly understood it, we wouldn't *want* to remove it. It's an essential part of God's goodness.

GOD'S WRATH IS REAL

If you take your Bible seriously at all, there's no denying the existence of God's wrath. The Old and New Testaments are filled with more than six hundred references to it. In the Psalms, David tells us that God is "angry with the wicked every day" (Ps 7:11 NLT).

This is another place many assume a big "gap" between the Old and New Testaments. God got a lot nicer in the New Testament. He grew up a little and came back to earth as God 2.0., Jesus-the-meek-and-mild.

Growing up, that's how I saw Jesus. I learned the gospel through "flannelgraph Jesus." We had cutout figures for almost every moment of his life: Jesus with sheep on his shoulders, bread in his hands, or two fingers lifted in blessing. We didn't have a "raining-down-judgment" Jesus, however. Nor can I recall a "flared-nostrils-and-a-bullwhip-in-his-hand" Jesus (Matt 21:12–17).

The wrath of God, however, was one of Jesus's primary teaching themes. He said, "Whoever rejects the Son will not see life, for God's wrath remains on them" (John 3:36). In *Why I Am Not a Christian*, skeptic Bertrand Russell admitted that the primary reason he couldn't believe Jesus was because he believed in hell and taught about it "in one verse after another . . . again and again." Russell called Christ's belief in the wrath of God "the one serious defect in Christ's moral character."[2]

The Pharisees didn't hate Jesus because of his effusive talk about God as the missing piece in their lives. They killed him because he told them that God's wrath was coming upon them (Matt 23:13–36).

GOD'S WRATH IS AN EXPRESSION OF HIS GOODNESS

On Mount Sinai, God revealed his wrath to Moses as a dimension of his goodness. When God passed before him in all his glory, he said, "I will make all my goodness before you." Not, "Now Moses, after I make all my goodness pass before you . . . you're going to see a little bit of my badness too," as if his wrath was the dark side of an otherwise good nature. God's wrath is an essential *part* of his goodness:

> I will make all my goodness pass before you and will proclaim before you my name "The LORD." . . . And the LORD descended in the cloud and . . . proclaimed, "The LORD, the LORD, a God merciful and gracious, slow to anger, and abounding in steadfast love and faithfulness, keeping steadfast love for thousands, forgiving iniquity and transgression and sin, but who will by no means clear the guilty, visiting the iniquity of the fathers on the children and the children's children, to the third and the fourth generation." (Exod 33:19–34:7 ESV)

His wrath is a natural extension of his love. That's because God is holy, and holiness demands justice. A world without justice would be a terrible world to live in.

Deep down, we agree. Don't we get angry when we see someone guilty of oppression or corruption or racism or lying get away with it? When the racist, the oppressor, or the abuser go free?

Miroslav Volf, a survivor of the oppression and genocide in Croatia, said that when you watch family and friends murdered in front of you, the only way to keep from going insane is to know that there is a God who is angry at what is happening and will one day restore justice. If your God doesn't possess the ability to feel wrath, he says, you will seethe with an insatiable desire for vengeance. Only when you believe that God has the sword in *his* hand can you lay it down from your own.[3]

Furthermore, when you truly love something, you hate whatever destroys it. When you love the cancer victim, you *hate* the cancer destroying her body. It is *because* I love my children that I can't ignore moral deficiencies in them that I know will harm them, such as dishonesty, cruelty, spite, laziness, or rebellion. I get angry when I see those traits in my kids—not *in spite* of my love for them but *because* I do! Left unchecked, they will make a relationship between us impossible. Sin, like a cancer, ruins God's good creation and destroys any chance of a relationship with him. So God hates it.

Just before God's encounter with Moses in Exodus 33, God demonstrated the "why" of his wrath through the ten plagues in Egypt. As a kid in Sunday school, I looked at the ten plagues as ten random curses that God unleashed on Egypt to vent his frustration, ten amazing practical jokes to cow Pharaoh into submission.

If God merely wanted to intimidate Pharaoh, there were much more efficient ways to do it. For example, Moses could have walked in to Pharaoh's court and delivered his message, and when Pharaoh said, "Why should I believe you?" he could have said, "Because I can levitate." Boom, levitation. Or he could have put the Darth Vader chokehold on Pharaoh. "I find your lack of faith . . . disturbing." Either of those would have gotten Pharaoh's attention.

But God did much more in these plagues than simply show off his power to Pharaoh. He demonstrated the power that *sin* had too. Moses called these plagues *signs*, which meant that the plagues illustrated a truth (Exod 8:23). In the plagues, we see creation systematically unravel. God turned the Nile into blood, which destroyed the natural ecosystem; out of the Nile fled the frogs; after the frogs died, the gnats came; from the gnats, painful disease, skin boils, etc. The message? Sin rips apart God's creation. In the creation account, God brought order out of chaos (Gen 1:2–4). In the plagues, sin drives a beautiful and orderly creation back into chaos!

Our culture, of course, spins the opposite narrative: sin leads to life and freedom. Never mind God's opinion; only *you* know what's right for you.

That narrative is a lie. Sin always leads to ruin. And because God is love, he cannot sit idly by and watch it happen. The opposite of love, it's said, is not hate, but *apathy*. Apathy means you don't care. Hate is actually an evidence of love—we only hate something when it threatens something we love. Just as we take radical measures to rid the person we love of the cancer we hate, God takes radical measures to rid his creation of injustice, greed, racism, exploitation, and perversity.

Without God's wrath, his goodness would not be that good.

Deep down, we long for a place where there is no more evil, no more injustice, no more tears or crying, which is exactly where God wants to take us (Rev 21:4). Wrath is a necessary part of the path to get us there.

But herein lies a dilemma: Aren't the people God loves the ones perpetuating evil? How then can heaven be a place without crying if *we* are there? Aren't we usually the ones who *cause* the crying? I think of how often *my* acts of selfishness have made someone else cry. If God takes me into heaven as I am, I will undoubtedly cause crying there, just as I have here. "No more tears in heaven" also means "no more J. D. Greear in heaven."

A heavenly place without heavenly citizens would be a paradise teetering on the brink of hell. To this dilemma, we will return.

GOD'S WRATH IS FIRST EXPERIENCED IN THE NATURAL CONSEQUENCES OF OUR CHOICES

Suppose my son comes into the kitchen and asks for a glass of milk. I tell him that the milk has gone bad and suggest he get a glass of juice instead. But he rolls his eyes and takes a gigantic swig from the milk carton anyway. As he gags on the congealed, odiferous lumps sliding down his throat, he can't rightfully say, "Dad, what have you done to me?" (Not that he *won't* say that. It's just that he can't *rightfully* say it.)

God's wrath first consists of allowing us to experience the natural consequences of our decisions. Theologians call this the "passive" dimension of God's wrath: we're the ones acting, not he. He simply stays out of the way and lets us experience the consequences of our choices.

This is what God is referring to when he says he will "[visit] the iniquity of the fathers on the children and the children's children, to the third and the fourth generation" (Exod 34:7 ESV). That can't mean that God will actively hold the kids morally accountable for the actions of their parents, since God says he doesn't do that (Ezek 18:19–20). What it means is that a parent's sin often has consequences in the lives of their children, sometimes for several generations into the future. Children's lives are changed if their dad commits tax fraud and goes to prison. It's not that God is actively punishing the child for the parent's sin, just that sin has natural consequences that affect everyone close to the sinner. This is the passive wrath of God.

The "active" wrath of God upon our sin—the thunderbolt of justice that strikes from heaven—operates as an extension of or conclusion to his passive wrath. It intensifies the natural consequences we have brought upon ourselves. For example, after Adam and Eve sinned, God punished them by casting them out of his presence. But hadn't they *already* hidden themselves from his presence? God was simply granting them what they had chosen for themselves (Gen 3:10, 22–24). Or think of Pharaoh, whom God judged by hardening his heart. Yet Exodus tells us Pharaoh had hardened his own heart several times already. God simply made his choice permanent (Exod 8:32; 9:12).

The wrath of God is a frightening reality, but it is only an extension of the choices we've made for ourselves. Hell starts as a *state* before it ends as a *place*.

That means when we experience the early, bitter stages of God's passive wrath, we are experiencing a dimension of his love and mercy. He is trying to wake us up. He is allowing us to taste some of the bitter consequences of our choices before they come to full, deadly, permanent fruition in our lives.

I know of a Christian leader who talks about experiencing God's mercy in the revelation of an inappropriate relationship that destroyed his ministry. The relationship had not yet progressed to adultery, but because he was so well known, the news of their inappropriate communication made headlines. He was publicly humiliated and had to step down. At first, he wondered why God had judged him so harshly, especially since he had not followed through with his sin. In time, he said, he came to see the exposure as God's mercy. God arrested his sin in its infancy before it could grow into something permanently destructive.

"Without the exposure," he said, "my sin may have grown to a point that would have permanently destroyed my family. Even worse, I may have never learned to hate my sin, which would have destroyed my soul."

Experiencing pain or humiliation because of your sin may *feel* like God's wrath, but it is actually the tender outworking of his compassion. He is trying to wake you up, showing you that sin takes you somewhere you don't want to go. As a friend of mine says, "He's not trying to pay you back, but bring you back."

GOD CHOSE TO LET HIS LOVE OVERCOME HIS WRATH

Even though God's wrath is good, right, and necessary, at the cross we see his compassion overcome it. He tells Moses that though his justice extends "to the *third and fourth* generation," his mercy extends to "*thousands* of generations." In other words, God's mercy is exponentially greater than his wrath, by at least a factor of 250!

When God looks at us, he feels two legitimate and conflicting passions—wrath and compassion. He loves us because we are his creatures. Yet he hates how we have trampled on his glory and destroyed his creation.

The wonder of the gospel is that at the cross God *chose* to let his love overcome his wrath. He didn't have to. One targum (an ancient Aramaic paraphrase of the Old Testament) translates Exodus 34:7 as our God is *"the one who makes anger distant and brings compassion near."* God's decision to act on his compassion, rather than his wrath, was his own free choice. He would have been right to let us experience wrath. But he chose to redeem us.

The apostle Peter says that the angels are genuinely baffled by the choice (1 Pet 1:12). The "math" of grace simply does not add up for them! Why did God choose compassion for us? Why not give us the godless eternity we asked for and start over with a new creation? Isn't that what happened with the angels? Nothing indicates that God gave them a chance to be redeemed after they rejected his authority.[4]

Paul expressed his own wonder at God's choice to show compassion:

> When we were still powerless, Christ died for the *ungodly.* Very rarely will anyone die for a righteous person. . . . But God demonstrates his own love for us in this: While we were *still sinners*, Christ died for us. . . . While we were *God's enemies*, we were reconciled to him through the death of his Son. (Rom 5:6–10, emphasis mine)

Notice that Paul doesn't call us "wayward children" or "confused sheep." That's because we weren't either of those things when God chose to redeem us. We were godless. Sinners. His enemies. His forgiveness is not like me forgiving my kids for reading with a flashlight after bedtime. It is more like me adopting into my family a terrorist who murdered one of my children.

Yes, our sin really was *that bad.*

Against the dark backdrop of our sin, the glory of God's compassion shines in blazing contrast. There truly is no greater wonder in the universe than God's love for us.

WE CAN ESCAPE GOD'S WRATH THROUGH CHRIST

The juxtaposition of God's wrath and compassion created a conundrum that baffled Jewish theologians for centuries: "The LORD, the LORD, a God merciful and gracious . . . forgiving iniquity and transgression and sin, but who will by no means clear the guilty" (Exod 34:6–7 ESV).

If God does not clear *the guilty*, then whose sin exactly is he forgiving when he forgives iniquity and transgression and sin? Aren't all those who sin, by definition, *guilty*? Moses probably left this encounter thinking, "Well, I don't see how this works, but that's how God says it is."

Fortunately for us, the Bible doesn't end at Exodus 34:7. Moses couldn't see it yet, but God was going to simultaneously punish the guilty *and* forgive them by transferring their guilt onto Jesus and punishing him in their place. Centuries after God's encounter with Moses, God again descended from heaven—this time not in a cloud but in an infant's body. He lived a sinless life but died a sinner's death. He would live the life of the righteous but die the death of the guilty.

In Christ, God did not overlook the guilt of the guilty; he poured it on a substitute—himself. As Isaiah says, "He was pierced for our transgressions, he was crushed for our iniquities. . . . The Lord has laid on him the iniquity of us all" (Isa 53:5–6). In Christ, guilt was punished, and we, the guilty, can be forgiven. God chooses to let his love overcome his wrath if we choose to receive his offer in Christ.

Deep down, each of us knows that a day of judgment is coming. Even if we cease believing in God, our consciences continue to tell us this day is coming. Playwright and atheist Arthur Miller, who wrote the famous *Death of a Salesman*, explained that he became an atheist in part because he was tired of feeling guilty. Even after his de-conversion, however, his feelings of guilt remained, only now he had no way of redressing them. "The bench was now empty," he explained, and so he began to look to audience approval for the validation he had once searched for in God.[5]

We all need someone to look at our lives and declare, "Not guilty!" If we kick God out of the courtroom, we'll just replace him with some other judge. No other judge, however, has the same authority or willingness to forgive.

The beauty of the gospel is that the One who has the right to condemn us has also made provision for our forgiveness. Even though we stand condemned before God, he tells us not to fear because he has taken our judgment onto himself. As Martin Luther put it, the voice of condemnation declares to our hearts, *You are guilty,* but God speaks with a louder voice in the gospel, *I have taken your sin.* So, when condemnation whispers, *You are finished,* we need only look to the cross to hear Jesus's triumphant answer: *No! It is finished.*

DO NOT IGNORE GOD'S SLOW-BUT-CERTAIN WRATH

There is one final thing we need to note about God's wrath from God's explanation to Moses: *it is coming.*

God told Moses that he was slow to wrath (Exod 34:6). At least, that's what it says in English. Personally, I think the Hebrew reads much better—literally it says, "God has long nostrils."[6] How do big noses indicate slowness to anger? Well, what happens when you get angry? Your nostrils flare. If you're quick-tempered, your flaring nostrils get going right away. Soon you're like a bull, raring to charge. But what do you do if you're trying to control your anger? Well, you close your mouth and breathe deeply through your nose slowly . . . while you say some serenity phrase to yourself like "goosfraba."[7]

God is righteously angry at sin, but he's not short-tempered. He doesn't want to pour out his wrath. He waits patiently, heartbroken and longing for our repentance.[8] The apostle Peter says this explains why there are such long gaps between when God pronounces judgment and when he finally brings it (2 Pet 3:3–9). It was more than one hundred years between the time God told Noah he was going to send the flood and the time it actually came. Why did he wait so long? Peter answers, because God "is patient . . . not wanting anyone to perish, but everyone to come to repentance" (v. 9).

Did you know that the oldest man ever to live was a walking parable about the "slowness" of God's wrath? Methuselah lived for 969 years (Gen 5:27). His name means "when he is dead, it shall be sent." If you add up the years in the genealogy around the flood, you'll see that Methuselah died in the year the flood came.

Peter goes on to explain that throughout human history, people have mistaken God's slowness to anger for its absence. Noah's generation assumed the flood wouldn't come, but it did. Today, people assume that Jesus's two-thousand-year absence means he's never coming back. But he is. As sure as you woke up this morning, he's returning. The only reason he delays, Peter says, is to give people another day to repent. For every nonbeliever who woke up this morning, God's hope is that today will be the day of their repentance.

He's calling you. Right now. He's using the pain, loneliness, and confusion in your life to draw you to himself. He has let you taste some of the bitterness of your sin to wake you up to your need for him. He's urging you to receive his offer of salvation, to escape from his coming wrath. He doesn't want to judge you. He wants to save you.

One summer during seminary, I worked a landscaping job with a group of men quite unlike the friends I had made at seminary. One of the men was a six-foot-six behemoth of a man we all called "Ivan." (This wasn't his real name, but he reminded us of Ivan Drago from *Rocky IV*.)

His language could have made a drunken sailor blush. I'm not a cusser myself, but some of the profanity strings he put together were quite creative, I had to admit. I tried to ignore it as much as I could, but one day he let out an invective that included several curses directed at God himself. I couldn't help myself. I had to say something. I blurted out, "You've got to stop that!" In that moment I felt bold, strong, and filled with the Holy Spirit, like John the Baptist of old. I put my finger right up in his face and said, "Ivan, one day you're going to stand before the judgment seat of God. And the last thing you'll want to have to answer for is cursing his name like that."

And then, at once, as quickly as he came, the Holy Spirit departed. And it felt like just me standing there, all alone. I turned and made my exit, a mixture of a mic drop and a squirrel scampering for safety. I heard big footsteps coming from behind me and braced for the worst.

But he wasn't angry. He started to get choked up.

"You seriously believe that?" he said.

"Yes," I told him. "The Bible says we all will stand before God and give an account for our lives."

"A few weeks ago, I got diagnosed with skin cancer," he replied. "And my wife and I are scared. I'm not sure what the future looks like for me . . . and here you are telling me about the judgment seat of God."

Ivan and I began a conversation about the gospel that extended through our lunch break and through every other break that day. At the end of our shift, we were standing in a parking lot when a car blazed through an intersection right behind us, colliding with another car and flipping onto its side. Ivan helped lift the car to rescue the young boy who was trapped inside. We both stood stunned as the first responders rushed in to help.

For a while, Ivan didn't say anything. Finally, he leaned over and said, "First, a skin cancer diagnosis. Then, you warning me about God's judgment. Now, I'm witness to an accident where a kid almost dies. . . . J. D., do you think God is trying to speak to me?"

"No, Ivan," I said. "I think God is *screaming* at you."

A few days later, Ivan gave his heart to Jesus.

God speaks to every one of us, pleading with us to flee to him from judgment. Maybe he's doing that with you right now. Maybe he's whispering to you through pain in your life, a troubled conscience, or fear about the future. These are all God's messengers of mercy to wake you up. Don't ignore them.

God didn't create you for wrath. He created you for relationship. He didn't design hell for you (Matt 25:41). He wants you to experience eternal happiness with him. The last person who wants you to experience the wrath of God is God! But he won't deprive you of the dignity of choice. He won't force you into eternal happiness. He'll extend pardon to all who will receive it. But you have to choose it.

I recently read about one of the most bizarre Supreme Court cases of all time—*United States v. Wilson, 1833*. The defendant, George Wilson, pled guilty to several counts of robbery and "endangering the life of a mail driver." This was apparently serious enough to warrant the death penalty, and Wilson was sentenced to be hanged. President Andrew Jackson chose to issue Wilson a full pardon, but Wilson, for reasons we will probably never know, refused to accept it.

The odd case went all the way to the Supreme Court, and this was their verdict:

> A pardon is an act of grace . . . which exempts the individual on whom it is bestowed from the punishment the law inflicts for a crime he has committed. . . . A pardon is a deed, to the validity of which delivery is essential, and delivery is not complete without acceptance. It may then be rejected, . . . and if it be rejected, we have discovered no power in a court to force it on him.[9]

It is true: God threatens terrible things for those who refuse to be happy in him. The tragedy of the human race is that many will die and go to hell with their pardon sitting on heaven's desk. We are free, as George Wilson did, to reject God's pardon.

But we don't have to, and God doesn't want us to. At the cross, he chose to overcome his wrath with mercy. You choose which attribute you'd rather experience. The choice is yours and yours alone: "Whoever believes in the Son has eternal life, but whoever rejects the Son will not see life, for God's wrath remains on them" (John 3:36).

If you have never done that, why not do it right now?

That choice is the beginning of a journey. A journey that plunges you into a bottomless well of love. A love great enough to overcome God's wrath. A love that even the most profound thinkers, under the inspiration of the Holy Spirit, found impossible to describe and even scandalous to explain.

CHAPTER 10

SCANDALOUS

We looked up from our chicken wings and cheese fries to see a slow trickle of women in their midthirties filling up the sports bar. We were in Ohio and had chosen an ideal spot, we believed, to watch the Cleveland Cavs lose the deciding game of the NBA finals. Everyone in there wore the requisite burgundy and blue. When the final buzzer sounded, the restaurant cleared out so fast it was like someone had yelled "fire!" That's when the migration of women dressed in parachute pants, tube tops, and jelly shoes began.

At first, it was just a handful of them. Then, dozens. Within the space of about twenty minutes, the entire restaurant was filled with women dressed in fashions I hadn't seen since the early '90s. My friend tapped me on the shoulder and told me to look out the window onto the street where there were—no exaggeration—at least five hundred women sauntering down the street like we were in some kind of 1980s zombie apocalypse.

I asked one of the ladies near our table, "What is going on?" She told me, "The New Kids on the Block reunion tour concert just ended!" While the Cavs were choking away the final, these ladies had been taking a sweet little trip down memory lane with the Now Middle-Aged Kids on the Block.

Probably 70 percent of those ladies had been convinced in

middle school that they were going to marry Donnie, the lead singer with the boyishly-cute-though-still-a-tough-guy persona. A friend told me that his wife may or may not have been in that group. She replied, "Oh, I remember it. All the girls tried to get to the front row so they could scream, 'I love you, Donnie!' Sure, you were only one of hundreds of girls, but you were convinced that your scream was going to be just a little bit louder than everyone else's, and Donnie was going to look over at you . . . and you'd have a split-second moment of enchantment. Later, a bouncer would find you and hand you a personal note from Donnie that said, 'You got the right stuff, baby. You're the reason why I sing this song.' And then you were going to get married and have cute little kids with floppy hair and live in Malibu."

Unless your name is Kim Fey or Jenny McCarthy, that never happened. Instead, you married Phil from accounting, a responsible man who is slightly overweight, balding, wears penny loafers, and drives a minivan.

Perhaps now you look at middle school girls dreaming the same thing about Justin Bieber or Hunter Hayes and think, "Sorry, sweetheart, it ain't goin' to happen." And maybe that comes with a hint of bitterness, but that's OK because you're discipling the next generation. Your duty is, as Donnie would say, to "shake them to wake them from this bad dream." Life is too short to be a groupie.

A groupie gives inordinate attention to someone who ignores them. Judah Smith says that one of the most mind-blowing things in Scripture is that we see God take this posture with the sinful human race.[1] Unlike groupies, however, God is not enamored with our greatness, nor is he desperate for our attention. He does not marvel at our brilliance, nor is he taken in by our beauty. We are sinners who do not deserve his tolerance, much less his affection! Yet, from the first pages of Genesis to the last chapters of Revelation, we see God reaching out to people who pay him no attention.

The apostle John exclaimed, "Behold what manner of love the

Father has bestowed upon us, that we should be called the children of God!" (1 John 3:1 NKJV). John chose one word to encapsulate all of God: love. "God is love" (1 John 4:8).

Discovering this love turns faith into passion (1 John 3:1–3; 4:19).

IMPOSSIBLE TO DESCRIBE

God's love surpasses any human analogy. It's greater than anything we can describe or comprehend.

The prophet Isaiah said that it's more likely that the mother of a newborn child would forget her baby than that God would forget us (Isa 49:15). When my wife and I had our first child, I was amazed by how in tune she was with that child. She would perk up in the middle of the night at the slightest whimper. I'd get up the next morning and say, "Wow, I guess Kharis slept through the night." To which my wife would roll her eyes and say, "Hardly. *You* slept through the night. She and I didn't." Eventually, I wised up and would say, "Oh yeah, I heard her too. . . . I just wanted to give you two that special time to bond." #dadoftheyear

God *can't* forget us, as Isaiah explains, because he has "engraved" us on the palms of his hands (Isa 49:16). He hears our slightest whimper. He even knows when a single hair falls from our heads. His nanny cam is always on.

Even this description falls short of communicating the magnitude of God's love. So, throughout Scripture, God uses stories—scandalous stories—to help us feel the remarkable extent of his love.

JONAH: FORGIVING THE UNFORGIVABLE

God told Jonah to go and preach salvation to the Ninevites. Jonah refused. Before we shake our heads in self-righteous dismay at Jonah, however, consider Jonah's history with the Ninevites.

The Ninevites were one of the cruelest civilizations in the ancient world. In a recently discovered library, archaeologists found the following statements made by Ninevite kings:

- "A pyramid of heads I reared in front of [the conquered king's] city."
- "Their corpses I formed into pillars; their youths and their maidens I burnt up in the flames."
- "I cut their throats like lambs. I cut off their precious lives [as one cuts] a string. Like the many waters of a storm, I made [the contents of] their gullets and entrails run down upon the wide earth. . . . Their hands I cut off."
- "I flayed him [referring to a conquered king]; his skin I spread upon the wall of the city."
- "I pierced his [another conquered king] chin with my dagger. Through his jaw I passed a rope, put a dog chain upon him, and kept him in a kennel in the city square."[2]
- "I tied them up and made them listen to the *Frozen* soundtrack both day and night."

I may have made that last one up. But you can see why Jonah was not eager to go plant a church in Nineveh. His response, if brash, is at least honest: *God, I don't want to go because I don't want these people to be saved. I want them to die.* Imagine the parents of a child killed in a terrorist bombing being told by God to go to the terrorists and tell them, "God says he forgives you and wants to shower mercy and blessing on you and your children." No wonder Jonah ran in the other direction.

So God sends a big fish to change Jonah's mind, and eventually Jonah reconsiders. Not because he felt differently about the Ninevites, but because he was tired of living inside a whale.

To Jonah's disappointment, the Ninevites heeded his sermon. They repented! God and all of heaven rejoiced, but Jonah was ticked: "O LORD, is not this what I said when I was yet in my country? That is why

I made haste to flee to Tarshish; for I knew that you are a gracious God and merciful [quoting from Exod 34:6–7], slow to anger and abounding in steadfast love, and relenting from disaster" (Jonah 4:1–2 ESV).

Jonah couldn't understand it. How could God possibly *love* the Ninevites? Didn't God know what they had done to his people? God not only showed compassion to Israel's oppressors, he made Jonah—whose people had suffered *personally* at their hands—deliver the message!

Why not send someone else?

Because God wanted Jonah to taste the outrageous extravagance of his love *toward Israel*. In preaching grace to the Ninevites, God gave Jonah a glimpse of his grace toward Jonah. Even though his sin was unspeakably wicked, God never stopped loving him either. Jonah had to experience great *personal* injustice to understand the scandal of God's love for sinners. Sinners like him.

HOSEA: LOVING THE UNLOVABLE

If you think Jonah's assignment was hard, you won't believe the one given to Hosea: "Go and marry a prostitute, so that some of her children will be conceived in prostitution. This will illustrate how Israel has acted like a prostitute by turning against the LORD and worshiping other gods" (Hos 1:2 NLT).

How would you like to get *that* assignment upon graduating from seminary? All your friends are getting preaching and teaching posts, and you are told to go and marry a prostitute. Not only that, but the prostitute Hosea marries is named "Gomer." If you are looking for biblical girl names for your daughter, I would not suggest "Gomer." I only know of one other Gomer, and he was a block-headed *dude* on *The Andy Griffith Show*.

Even so, Hosea obeyed God. And he didn't just go through the formalities, either. He genuinely tried to love Gomer and build a family with her. But Gomer soon returned to her old ways. She eventually left him for another man, a man who abused her.

Hosea pleaded with her to come back, but, insanely, she didn't. He even gave the man she lived with money to take care of her! Eventually, her "lover" got tired of her and sold her back into the sex-slave trade.

Then God appeared to Hosea with a second assignment: *Go buy her back!* "The LORD said to me, 'Go again, love this woman who is . . . an adulteress, even as the LORD loves the children of Israel, though they turn to other gods'" (Hos 3:1 ESV).

Keep in mind that this is not a parable. Hosea was a real person. He felt the same thing we'd feel in that situation: "Buy her back? But she scorned and humiliated me the first time. Why would I do that *again?*"

Hosea went to the auction.

Gomer stood before the crowd with the other slaves, stripped naked so potential buyers could see what they were bidding on. There among them stood Hosea, her rightful husband, in line with a group of men interested only in hiring her out for sex. What Hosea did, by the way, was not required by Hebrew law. In Leviticus, God said that a man in Hosea's situation had every right to divorce her or even have her stoned for unfaithfulness! Furthermore, purchasing Gomer this second time evidently broke Hosea financially, because thirty shekels was the going price of a slave in those days and Hosea could only come up with fifteen. The rest of the price he had to pay in kind (Hos 3:2).

Why did God put Hosea through this humiliation? Because there are certain dimensions of God's love that are better *experienced* than *explained.* We are like Nineveh, the forgiven unforgivable. We are also like Gomer, the loved unlovable. God was well within his legal rights to walk away from us. The price required to get us back would cost Jesus his very life.

God was saying to Hosea, "Hosea, you and I have both given our hearts to people who will utterly reject us. We will spend our years chasing after them. Until you experience that personally you won't grasp the magnificence of my love."

God then laments—in what might be the most remarkable verse in the entire Old Testament—

> Oh, how can I give you up, Israel?
> How can I let you go? . . .
> My heart is torn within me! (Hos 11:8 NLT)

How can I let you go? God has bound up his happiness in ours. He loves us so deeply that he can't just walk away from us, no matter how deeply our sin wounded him. Theologian J. I. Packer summarizes that truth this way: "By his own free voluntary choice, God will not know perfect and unmixed happiness again till he has brought every one of his children to heaven."[3]

Gomer's name, though not pleasant to our ears, means "completion" in Hebrew. God's happiness (by his own choice) will not be *complete* again until he saves us. Hers may not be a beautiful name, but it conveys a beautiful truth. Reflecting on that truth, Donald Grey Barnhouse writes,

> The pursuing love of God is *the greatest wonder in the spiritual universe.* When we see this love at work through the heart of Hosea we may wonder if God is really like that. But he is. Think about it: Many years later he would give man the trees of the forest and the iron in the ground. . . . He gave them the ability to form that iron into nails, and to fashion those trees into a cross. . . . Then he stretched out his hands upon that tree and allowed us to nail him there, and in so doing he took our sins upon himself. *This is our God, and there is no one else like him.*[4]

THE PRODIGAL FATHER: PURSUING THE DESERTER

In the Gospel of Luke, Jesus told a story about a wealthy farmer whose son came to him and said, "Dad, I hate living here, and I'm tired of you. Give me my inheritance. I'm leaving." An inheritance—then as well as now—is what you got when your parents died, so his demand for the inheritance was a way of saying, "Dad, I don't care about you at all. You are only good for your money."

He then took the family inheritance and blew it on parties and prostitutes. In the process, he destroyed not only the family fortune but also the family name. Jewish law said that such a son could be killed. More often than not, however, Jewish families in such circumstances would conduct a ceremony called the *kezazah*— literally, the "cutting off"—in which they pronounced the runaway functionally dead. After the *kezazah*, the community had nothing more to do with the wayward child.[5]

The father in this story never performed that ceremony. Instead, he waited gazing mournfully each evening in the direction his son had gone.

Then one day, he saw him. He caught sight of his son coming over the distant horizon. Poor. Worn out. Hurt. And this stately, graceful father began to do something that shocked everyone—he began to run toward his son.

Older Jewish men in the first century did not run. Running was considered undignified, especially because you had to lift the front of your robe and expose your knees to really get moving. But this father no longer cared about dignity.

Almost every North Carolinian has seen the iconic video of Jimmy Valvano, the head coach of North Carolina State University's men's basketball team, running around the court like a crazy man after NC State overcame unbelievable odds to win their first NCAA national championship in 1983. If you watch the video, he literally looks like a madman. But had you told Valvano at the time, "What are you doing? You are embarrassing yourself! Have some dignity!" he would likely have said, "Dignity? Who cares! We just won our first national championship!"

Had you said to this father, "Stop it. You're embarrassing your-self," I expect he would have said, "Embarrassment? Who cares! My son is coming home!"

God's love for us is so passionate and intense that he put aside his dignity to save us. As Hebrews says, for the joy set before him he "scorned" (or disregarded) the shame of the cross (Heb 12:2). All he could think about on the way to Calvary was the joy of rescuing us.

This story is commonly called "The Story of the Prodigal Son," because people assume that "prodigal" means "runaway." But prodigal means "reckless" or "wasteful." As Tim Keller points out, the most reckless character in this story is not the son blowing his inheritance; it's the Father with his forgiveness.[6]

SOME THINGS ARE BETTER EXPERIENCED THAN EXPLAINED

Through these three shocking stories, we get to behold the scandalous love of God for us. If you have felt the weightiness of this love, even for a moment, you know that it defies description. No wonder the silver-tongued orator Charles Spurgeon could only say:

> If there is one [subject] which . . . makes me go back from this platform utterly ashamed of my poor feeble words, it is this subject. This love of Christ is the most amazing thing under heaven, if not in heaven itself.[7]

And Martin Luther, the great Reformer, whose theological writings constitute their own library, said:

> If we had a full understanding of this love of God for men, a joy so great would come to us from this recognition that we would promptly die because of it. From this we see how great our feebleness is, how truly dull our hearts, since few taste even a few drops of this immense joy, not to mention the whole ocean.[8]

But there is yet another story—one greater still—that demonstrates the extravagance of God's love for us. And when that story unfolded, even the angels stood speechless.

CHAPTER 11

HOW TO CONFUSE
AN ANGEL

What does it take to impress an angel? There's not much angels haven't seen, after all. They had a front row seat at creation. They have seen God make a donkey talk. They filled the heavens with praise at the birth of the baby Jesus and rolled the stone away from Jesus's tomb.

The apostle Peter tells us there is one thing, however, that still blows their minds, one thing that leaves them in hushed silence:

God's love for the rebellious human race.

As we saw in the previous chapter, Scripture teaches us the love of God with stories that scandalize us. There's one more that seems to have left even the angels speechless. It occurs in Mark's Gospel, and I think it's the most mysterious passage in all of Scripture. Mark recounts Jesus's final, private moments with his Father before his death. It's the kind of passage I like to approach on my knees.

THE FINAL MOMENTS

After Judas left to betray Jesus, Jesus retreated to a favorite spot, the garden of Gethsemane, to spend time alone with his Father before the cross. Instead of finding solace, however, Mark tells us he was overcome with horror (Mark 14:33).

Scholars say that the word Mark used to describe Jesus's feelings in that moment indicates the kind of feeling you'd have if you encountered something so terrible you couldn't describe it in words—like coming home one evening to find your family mutilated. The emotion was so overpowering that Jesus, who is not one prone to exaggeration, said he almost *died* from it (14:34).

SCARED TO DEATH

What could have been so frightening that merely the sight of it almost killed Jesus? He stood toe-to-toe with demons without flinching. To Jesus, hurricane force winds could be calmed like toddlers. Even the untimely death of his friends, which *saddened* Jesus, didn't *frighten* him.

What could frighten the Son of God?

Actually, it's what Jesus *hadn't* seen that scared him. Throughout his life, whenever Jesus called out to his Father, the Father answered him with warmth and tenderness, sometimes even affirming him publicly (Matt 3:17; John 12:28). This time, however, Jesus was met with silence. Three times in a row (Mark 14:41).

Hearing nothing from his Father, Jesus stumbled back to his disciples and asked *them* to stay awake with him (14:37). *This is Jesus*—the one who commanded the wind and the waves—so weak that he's looking for someone, anyone, to lean on.

He felt alone. Abandoned.

More than that, he felt *rejected* by his Father. One thing I've learned about rejection is that the closer you are to someone, the more painful their rejection feels. Over the years, I have received my share of angry letters from people I've never met. They often say unkind things. But they seldom bother me because I don't have a relationship with them.

If I were to get such a letter from my father, however, telling me that *he* was ashamed of me, that would be different. We are close, and I have lived for over forty years now in the assurance of his love. Losing his affection would be unspeakably painful. If losing the love of my earthly father would feel like that, what was it like for Jesus to lose the perfect love of his eternal Father?

Luke tells us that Jesus was so crushed by his Father's abandonment that he began to sweat great drops of blood (Luke 22:44)—a condition doctors call *hematidrosis*, in which the capillaries in your face burst from intense strain.

A friend of mine spent the day at the pool with his family. When they packed up their kids in the car to go home, he noticed that their three-year-old wasn't with them. He raced back to the pool and found his son lying unconscious at the bottom. He pulled him out, began CPR, and managed to revive him. They rushed the boy to the emergency room, where he stayed overnight for observation.

The following morning, my friend noticed dozens of small purple blotches like tiny bruises all over his son's face. The doctor explained that the most likely explanation was that as his son realized he was drowning, he had screamed so forcefully for his father that the capillaries in his face burst.

In Gethsemane, we see Jesus—who spoke the worlds into existence, walked on top of angry waves, calmed the fiercest storms, cast out the vilest demons, healed the gravest diseases, and brought the dead back to life—so horrified that his blood vessels burst. The pain of the Father's abandonment was more than his physical heart could bear.

Long before the nails pierced Jesus's hands, the journey to the cross was underway. The Father had begun to turn his face away. New Testament scholar William L. Lane describes this moment in Gethsemane as "the horror of one who lived wholly for the Father, who came to be with his Father for a brief interlude before his death and found hell rather than heaven open before him."[1] In that moment, God gave to Jesus a glimpse of what he was about to go through on the cross, where he would cry out in agony, "My God, my God, why have you forsaken me?" (Matt 27:46).

In this one moment, Jesus experienced a taste of hell for us, because that's what hell is—*total abandonment by God.*

No wonder the angels watched in stunned silence. The Son of God, ruler of the heavens, was horrified to the point of death; God, who spoke the worlds into existence, so weak he seemed unable to stand on his own.

KNOWING THE UNKNOWABLE

Reflecting on this passage, the eighteenth-century theologian Jonathan Edwards asked: *Why* did the Father show all this to Jesus *before* he actually went to the cross? What if this vision had horrified Jesus to the point he couldn't go through with his sacrifice?

The only answer is that God was letting us *see* Jesus go to the cross *voluntarily*, knowing full well what he was about to experience. Seeing him encounter this reality and go through with it anyway gives us an even clearer understanding of his love for us. For the same reason, Jesus refused the narcotic offered to him at the cross (Matt 27:34). He was displaying the greatness of his love for us (Rom 5:8).

Luke tells us that at the end of Jesus's time in the garden, an angel came to minister to him. How would you like to be the angel who received *that* assignment? What would you say to "minister" to Jesus in that moment? We don't know what the angel said. But we know that when Jesus left the garden of Gethsemane, he did so with joy: "For the joy set before him he endured the cross, scorning its shame, and sat down at the right hand of the throne of God" (Heb 12:2).

In the garden, Jesus was crushed with sorrow to the point of death, but he walked toward the cross buoyant with joy. What was the joy set before him?

The Father's approval?

The adoration of angels?

Rule over the universe?

He certainly would receive all these things, but he had all these things *before* he went to the cross.

The one thing he didn't have—the one thing he *couldn't* have unless he went to the cross—was you. Isaiah says that we are so precious to God, so dear, so cherished, that Jesus was willing to go through the horrors of the cross—hell itself—to buy us back (Isa 43:4). We were a large part of the joy set before him. As Isaac Watts put it,

> See from his head, his hands, his feet,
> sorrow and love flow mingled down!
> Did e'er such love and sorrow meet,
> or thorns compose so rich a crown![2]

The angels could only look on with wonder. They could come up with no explanation for why God would continue to love a race that had rejected, scorned, and humiliated him. Even now, Peter tells us, "angels long to look into these things" (1 Pet 1:12). They yearn to peer into the deeper mysteries of the gospel, and the more they look, the more they are amazed. And now, as they stand before God's throne crying "Holy, Holy, Holy," they do so in even greater admiration. Heaven itself can scarcely contain their passion. How much more should you and I stand amazed in his presence?

Some things, as we saw in the last chapter, cannot be properly explained in words; they must be *experienced* to be known. On the subject of God's love, our tongues fall silent, our pens go down, and our eyes gaze upward in worship. That's the only right response to the cross.

Even Paul felt his inadequacy to convey the magnitude of God's love. In the Letter to the Ephesians, after explaining the gospel in great detail for three full chapters, he prays that the Father would give the Ephesians the "Spirit of wisdom and revelation" so that they might "grasp how wide and long and high and deep is the love of Christ . . . that surpasses knowledge" (Eph 1:17; 3:18–19). He knows that the real magnitude of God's love is not something he can communicate in words. He wants the Ephesians to experience something personally that cannot be adequately conveyed propositionally. It's an experience, not an education, that he wants them to have.

Notice how he prays that they would *know* something that *surpasses knowledge*. It's like the difference between knowing that honey is sweet and actually tasting it. The tongue then knows what it feels inadequate to explain.

Experiential knowledge of the love of God like this yields three things: confidence, passion, and compassion.

CONFIDENCE IN LIFE

In the garden of Gethsemane, we see that Jesus did not forsake us even when hell was squeezing the life out of him. ("Gethsemane" literally means "oil press.") We can be confident that if Jesus did not leave us in *his* darkest hour, he won't leave us in our darkest hours either.

As I mentioned earlier, I don't always understand everything God is doing in my life. What I do know is that if Jesus did not forsake me in the garden of Gethsemane, he won't forsake me now.

This gives me incredible confidence in life. My standing before God is based on his perfect love and nothing more.

Many times we base our understanding of how God feels about us on how we are feeling. If we do that, we'll never *feel* secure. If we base it on how well our life is going, we'll feel loved when things are going well and forsaken when they're not. But if we base our confidence on what we see at the cross, we stand on a secure foundation. Even in our darkest moments, we'll know that his love supports us, weaving everything together for good.

After what we saw him willingly go through in Gethsemane, can we really doubt his love for us?

PASSION IN WORSHIP

Those who understand the extravagant price Jesus paid to save them can't respond casually. Either he is the Savior to whom we owe everything, or someone has told us a stupendous lie. It has to be one or the other. We must either reject him as a delusion or worship him as our Savior. There is no third alternative.

Suppose you come home one day to find a friend sitting on your front porch. Your friend informs you that while you were out, someone you owed money to came to collect your debt. But your friend says not to worry now because he paid the debt for you. How would you respond?

Well, it depends on how much they paid. If it was to the mailman, who said you were twenty-eight cents short on postage, you might clap your friend on the back and say, "Thanks." But if your friend says, "It was the mafia. Your gambling debts finally caught up to you. You owed thirty million dollars, and two guys were here to either collect the money or send you to sleep with the fishes," then a clap on the back and a casual "Thanks" will not suffice. A better response would be to fall on your face before your friend and say, "Command me."[3]

What kind of response should the sacrifice of Jesus elicit from us? The hymn writer expresses it perfectly:

> Were the whole realm of nature mine,
> that were a present far too small—
> love so amazing, so divine,
> demands my soul, my life, my all![4]

Jesus didn't die so we could play church. He didn't die to be our source of serenity in a busy life. He didn't endure the cross so we could huddle together in small groups and bemoan the deterioration of our culture.

He died to turn us into white-hot worshipers and world-transformers.

Jesus is not a safety net, a relief valve, an assistant, or a divine butler. He's a God whose glory and love deserve our utmost allegiance. The cross demands that we either offer our lives to him totally, without restrictions, or that we walk away from him in disgust, dismissing him as history's biggest fool. David Platt says, "[Jesus] is worthy of more than church attendance and casual association; he is worthy of total abandonment and supreme adoration."[5]

Is your life a worthy response to the gospel?

Does what you are doing with your life warrant the magnitude of his sacrifice?

Is what you are *living for* worth him *dying for*?

COMPASSION FOR OTHERS

An experience with the love of God, the apostle John says, will also change our attitude toward *others* (1 John 4:19).

Imagine that a friend showed up thirty minutes late to meet you at a coffee shop. As he walked in he said, "I'm so sorry I am late. You will not believe what happened to me on the way here! As I was getting into my car, a grand piano dropped from the sixteenth floor of an apartment building I was parked next to and landed right on my head. It made a huge mess, and it took me a while to find my keys because they had been knocked out of my hand. That's why I'm late."

Your reaction to your friend would be, "Uhhh ... I'm pretty sure you're lying. If you had been hit by a grand piano falling from sixteen stories up, you would look different. You'd walk different. You'd *talk* different. *Everything* about you would be different. There's no way you could get hit with that kind of force and stay the same."

There's no way we can experience the magnitude of gospel love and stay the same. Everything about us will be different. When we have really been impacted by God's love, Jesus's command in Luke 6:36, "Be merciful, just as your Father is merciful," becomes natural to us. Those who experience mercy become merciful.

Do radical measures of mercy characterize your life? Do you give generously? Do you forgive quickly? Do you talk constantly about the grace you've found in Jesus?

If not, it might be that you have never felt the weight of gospel on your heart. You need God to open the eyes of your heart to the love he displayed on the cross. It's probably not more facts you need to learn, but a reality you need to *feel*, a reality that only the Holy Spirit can open for you. The good news is that what Paul prayed for the Ephesians, you can pray for yourself. God wants to open your eyes (Eph 1:17–18; 3:16–19).

According to Peter, the angels stare with wonder at the love God showed to rebellious sinners at the cross. These same angels are now watching you. Do they see your life as a worthy response to the awesome love God displayed for you at the cross?

CHAPTER 12

CATCHING FIRE

When my oldest daughter was a toddler, she loved balloons. So for her third birthday party I blew up fifty red balloons. It was not an easy feat, but I was pretty excited about how excited she would be when she saw them.

When she walked into the party, however, she looked confused. She picked up one of the balloons and said, "Daddy, what's wrong with these balloons? They are broken. They don't float in the air like the ones from Red Robin" (which were helium balloons). Scrambling to salvage the moment, I explained that my balloons were better than the ones that float . . . because we could play games with them, like seeing who could keep their balloon in the air the longest by smacking it upward.

She didn't buy it. She wanted the ones that float on their own. Thanks, Red Robin.

If you blow up a balloon with your breath, the only way to keep it afloat is by smacking it continually. The moment you stop, the balloon will drop back down to the ground. Fill that same balloon with helium, however, and it soars on its own—no smacking required.

In chapter 5, "Untouchable Holiness," we saw that when it comes to our walk of faith, God wants believers who soar spiritually without the need for continual "smacking." He wants our hearts to be so captivated by his love, so amazed by who he is, that we couldn't imagine anything we'd *rather* do than please him. God is not just after *obedience*, but a whole new kind of obedience, an obedience fueled by *desire*. He is not content to compel our behavior with threats of punishment or promises of blessing. He wants people who seek him because they love him, who do righteousness because they delight in it.

But how can he create these kinds of desires in our hearts?

BEHOLDING AND BECOMING

Moses's encounter with God at Mount Sinai gives us the answer. When Moses *beheld* the glory of God, his face began to glow.

> And when Moses came down from Mount Sinai, . . . he was not aware that his face was radiant because he had spoken with the Lord. When Aaron and all the Israelites saw Moses, his face was radiant, and they were afraid to come near him. . . . When Moses finished speaking to them, he put a veil over his face. (Exod 34:29–33)

You can't experience God that closely and not show the effects. In Moses's case, his face actually radiated—as if lit by some inner fire.

The apostle Paul said that what happened to Moses gives us a picture of the transformation that happens in our hearts when we behold the glory of God in the face of Jesus Christ (2 Cor 3:18). As God opens our eyes to behold his glory in the story of Jesus, our hearts begin to glow with faith and love.

Until God opens our eyes to see his glory, all the changes we try to make in our lives will be short-lived. Just as no amount of smacking can transform the air in the balloon into helium, no amount of smacking ourselves with rules and regulations will make us love God. Love *for* God grows *in* us, the apostle John said, as we behold the love *of* God *toward* us: "We love because he first loved us" (1 John 4:19). Beholding leads us to becoming.

This is another thing I was missing in my faith. I was trying to develop a love for God by obedience to a command, as if I had the resources to obey that command. No matter how fervently I told my soul to love God, I couldn't make my soul do it. I experienced what Martin Luther called the "dilemma" of the Great Commandment: God commands us to do something that can't be commanded by commanding us to love him. If you love something, you don't need to be commanded to love it, and if you don't love it, no *command* can change that.[1]

Does God really delight in people who serve him begrudgingly? I'm surprised at how often we assume he'd be happy with that kind of service.

Would you want to be with someone who loved you only out of obligation?

During my senior year of high school, I dated a girl from a rival high school. On paper, she was perfect. The problem was there seemed to be very little romantic "magic" between us. No fireworks. I was going out of state to college, and I wasn't sure what to do. We didn't seem serious enough to warrant a breakup, but I didn't want to try to keep the relationship going eight hundred miles away. Unsure of what to do, I did the mature thing. I avoided the question.

We wrote a few times that first semester, but neither of us brought up the status of our relationship. Unfortunately, Facebook hadn't been invented yet, so I couldn't just log on and see whether she had changed our relationship status.

When I went home for Christmas, we arranged a time to get together. The day before our date, I had a sudden, alarming thought: Am I supposed to get her a Christmas present? It was, after all, a couple of days before Christmas.

My dilemma was this: If she got me a Christmas present and I didn't have one for her, I'd look like a thoughtless dolt. But what if I got her one and she didn't give me one? I'd have wasted fifty dollars on a girl fading from my life. It all feels so complicated sometimes.

I decided I'd better play it safe and get her *something*, at least to have as a backup. So I ran into a mall on the way to her house and looked for a store that might have something. . . . The first store I came to was a sporting goods store, and there I saw it—the absolute perfect gift: a snow skiing neck warmer. It said ADIDAS in really big letters across it, so you knew it was quality. It was only seven dollars—the kind of gift that says, "You're really special, and I like you a lot."

Perfect! If she gave me a present, I'd give her this little gem, and if she didn't give me anything, that puppy was mine!

I wrapped up the woolen treasure and put it under the seat of my car. When I arrived at her house, she came to the door, and the first thing out of her mouth was, "I bought you a Christmas present!"

Proudly, I said, "I got you one too!"

She ran back to her Christmas tree and pulled out a beauti-fully wrapped package. Nervously, I opened it, and was dismayed to see—not a pair of socks, an air freshener for my car, or a package of beef jerky—an expensive-looking sweater. Not good.

She looked at me expectantly and said, "So . . . where's my gift?"

Suddenly the pathetic neck-sock I had stuffed in a box under the seat of my car didn't seem quite so "perfect." I scrambled.

"Uhhh . . . I just realized I left yours back at my house!" I said, thinking that was a safe maneuver. I could always buy a new gift on the way home and then mail it to her.

She said, "Well, let's swing by your house and pick it up! I want to see your parents anyway."

"This is what the judgment of God feels like," I thought.

When we walked into my house, I asked her to wait in the liv-ing room. I pulled my mom aside and asked, "Was there anything you were planning to give Christy (my sister) that she doesn't know about yet?"

My mom said, "Why?"

I said, "I am not entertaining questions at this point."

Graciously, my mom found a nice, equivalently valued gift intended for my sister. We put my "girlfriend's" name on it, and I took it in to her and said, confidently, "Here's your gift."

Somehow, I pulled the whole thing off and, to my knowledge, she never knew. Hopefully, she never reads this book. If she does, I live in France now. But do you think if she'd known the real circumstances, she would have felt good about the gift?

Of course not. She probably wouldn't even have taken it, and our dating relationship would have ended right there. No one wants to be loved out of obligation.

For some reason, we think God is different. We assume he delights in our begrudging obedience and doesn't care *why* we obey, so long as we do.

Be serious! Dutiful, begrudging obedience is as distasteful to God as it is to us.

A transformed heart can't come from a list of commands. It takes something greater.

CHANGED BY A LOOK

Moses's face glowed because of what he saw, not how he lived. Only when we experience the glory of God like Moses did will we glow like he did.

"Great," you may say. "So where exactly can I get a vision of God like this? As far as I know, he's not appearing on mountains in my area."

As we saw, the apostle Paul explained that we encounter the same glory of God—to an even greater degree—in Jesus. With an unveiled face, we see the beauty of God's glory in the life and teaching of Jesus.

It is worth noting that Moses's encounter with the glory of God was as much about what he *heard* as what he *saw*. The author of Exodus tells us that when God passed in front of Moses, Moses *heard* God proclaiming his name:

> Then the LORD came down in the cloud and stood there with him and proclaimed his name, the LORD. And he passed in front of Moses, proclaiming, "The LORD, the LORD, the compassionate and gracious God, slow to anger, abounding in love and faithfulness, maintaining love to thousands, and forgiving wickedness, rebellion and sin. Yet he does not leave the guilty unpunished." (Exod 34:5–7)

In the same way, our hearts begin to glow with worship when we *hear* God's Spirit declaring Jesus's name to us, making his holiness, justice, love, and glory come alive in our hearts. It's not that we learn new facts about God. Facts we may already know suddenly become real and personal to us. Almost everything God said to Moses in that moment on the mountain Moses already knew—in a factual sense. In that moment, *he felt* the beauty of God's glory in a new and personal way.

In the same way, the Spirit of God opens our eyes to how wide and high, how long and deep is the love of God for us. In these moments, what we know with our heads becomes real to our hearts. Sin begins to lose its power over us. We experience "all the fullness of God" (Eph 3:19).

D. Martyn Lloyd-Jones compared this experience to a father walking along the road with his young son. As they're walking, the father suddenly picks up his son, spins him around, kisses him, and says, "Son, you know that I love you, and I'm so proud you are my boy!" In that moment, the boy is not *legally* any more his son than he was the moment before. But in that moment, the boy *feels* his sonship in a new way.[2]

So it is with God's presence. The fullness of the Spirit makes us *feel* the love of the gospel. Our acceptance in Christ goes from being a doctrine to a warm embrace. And just as Moses's face glowed from the experience, so our souls radiate with the joy and love of Christ.

That's what was missing from my faith. It had nothing to do with not trying hard enough. It had to do with failing to behold the glory of God displayed in the gospel.

Maybe that's where you are too. Maybe it's not something *new* that you need to learn, or some new habit you need to incorporate into your lifestyle. You need the Spirit of God to help you see Jesus more clearly.

The good news is that this is a prayer God loves to answer.

SOARING SPIRITUALLY

Victorious, passionate Christian living is the result of finally seeing God for who he is—standing humbled before the heights of his holiness and awestruck at the depths of his love. Then, and only then, will we soar spiritually.

If we can't escape the powers of sin, it's not because our wills are too weak but because the presence of God feels so distant. I was once invited to lead a Bible study for one of the fraternities at the University of North Carolina at Chapel Hill. I asked what subject they'd like me to cover, and (surprising no one) they said, "sexual temptation."

As I was leading the study, I made the offhand comment that they could turn on and off their sexual desires like a light switch. You should have seen the look on the faces of those nineteen-year-old fratties when I said that! One of them said, "Bro, we know our body changes as we get older, but we had no idea we'd feel that way at . . . forty?"

I explained that age had nothing to do with it. This statement was as true for them as it was for me.

One said, "Pastor, with all due respect, you're out of your mind."

"I'll prove it," I countered. "Say you are at your girlfriend's house, and things get pretty serious. One thing is leading to another. I don't know what y'all call it now because I'm not cool anymore, but when I was in college it had something to do with a baseball diamond. It's the point of no return. All systems are go. The train has left the station."

They nodded understandingly, and someone said, "That's what we're talking about. At that point, there is no way to turn back."

I said, "OK, now imagine that at just that moment, when you feel like there is no turning back . . . in walks that girl's Navy Seal father who has just returned from a tour of duty in Afghanistan. Off like a light switch."

They all stared at me silently for a moment, and then one turned to his friend and said, "Yeah, that's a good point."

I asked, "What happened in that moment? Did your sexual desires just evaporate? Did you cease being attracted to her? No, your strong desire for her was brought under control by an *even stronger* desire—specifically, the desire to stay alive.

"Your problem with sexual temptation is not that your sexual desires are too strong, but that your sense of the presence of God is too weak."

If you want to overcome sin, don't focus on shrinking your temptations; focus on enlarging your view of God.

The apostle Paul explains that *seeing* the largeness of God's grace "teaches us to say 'No' to ungodliness and worldly passions, and to live self-controlled, upright and godly lives in this present age" (Titus 2:12).

Seeing is the prerequisite to *doing*. In *beholding* is the power for *becoming*.

UNSTOPPABLE FAITH

Stephen, an ordinary guy, stood bound before a group of religious leaders who were seething with rage, stones in their hands, ready to martyr him. They demanded he cease speaking about Jesus.

But he, full of the Holy Spirit, gazed into heaven and saw the glory of God, and Jesus standing at the right hand of God. . . . They cried out with a loud voice and stopped their ears and rushed together at him. Then they cast him out of the city and stoned him. And as they were stoning Stephen, he called out, "Lord Jesus, receive my spirit." And falling to his knees he cried out with a loud voice, "Lord, do not hold this sin against them." And when he had said this, he fell asleep. (Acts 7:55–60 ESV)

Stephen went to his death joyfully. He wasn't merely fulfilling his obligations. His face glowed like an angel's (Acts 6:15). As he was being stoned, his spirit soared above the pain racking his body, forgiving his murderers with a compassion almost too tender to believe.

Where did he get the power to die like this? Where did Stephen's glow come from?

Just as with Moses, it came from what he saw: "But he, full of the Holy Spirit, gazed into heaven and saw the glory of God, and Jesus standing at the right hand of God" (v. 55). As Stephen looked up toward Jesus, he saw something remarkable. Every other place in the New Testament that we see Jesus at the right hand of God, he's sitting (Heb 10:12; Mark 16:19). But here, as Stephen dies, Jesus stands. Why?

Jesus was honoring Stephen. He was standing to receive him home. Everyone else in that moment called Stephen a heretic. Jesus stood and called him "Son."

They said, "You deserve to die." Jesus said, "Well done, my good and faithful servant."

The voices in front of Stephen were drowned out by the face of the One on the throne. And in that moment, Stephen decided that Jesus's approval was better than life. Stephen then said, "Lord Jesus, receive my spirit," and "Lord, do not hold this sin against them" (Acts 7:59–60). Where have you heard those statements before?

They are the same ones Jesus uttered from the cross: "Into your hands I commit my spirit," and "Father, forgive them, for they do not know what they are doing" (Luke 23:46, 34).

In Stephen's final moments, as he demonstrated a courage that takes your breath away, he was thinking about Jesus's death on the cross for him. He wasn't questioning the fairness of his persecution or panicking that the situation had spun out of control. He was overwhelmed by Jesus's power and grace. As the rocks pelted the life out of his body, Stephen's face glowed with passion and his soul radiated with compassion—not because he thought these were the ways he was *supposed* to feel, but because his heart had been so captivated by Jesus's love and grace that these were the ways he *couldn't help* but feel.

In the Christian life, the fire to do comes from one place: being soaked in the fuel of what has been done.[3] Whatever your circumstances, look up to Jesus, and let the Holy Spirit fill your heart with the wonder of his name. As you embrace your heavenly Father's eternal love for you, love for him will begin to radiate from your heart with a passion that will turn the world upside down. This vision, not new resolutions, is where it begins.

Maybe at this point you feel some of the old doubts coming back. You want to believe in his love, but if God is really so loving, why are you hurting? Why doesn't he come and fix your situation? Where is he in a world of such great need?

To overcome these questions, we need to understand one of the most basic facts of the universe, one that Stephen and every other world-transformer has understood well: *it's not about you.*

PART 3

BOLD FAITH IN A BIG GOD

"Aslan," said Lucy, "You're bigger."

"That is because you are older, little one," answered he.

"Not because you are?"

"I am not. But every year you grow, you will find me bigger."

C. S. LEWIS, *PRINCE CASPIAN*[1]

CHAPTER 13

IT'S NOT ABOUT YOU

Nicolaus Copernicus never intended to turn the world upside down. He wasn't even a professional astronomer. He was a physician who studied mathematics, politics, economics, and—only in his spare time—astronomy. But as he applied the same rigorous disciplines of observation to astronomy that he used in math and medicine, he noticed something that bothered him.

For centuries, astronomers had accepted the "Ptolemaic" understanding of the universe, in which the earth was believed to sit motionless at the center, surrounded in concentric circles by the moon, the sun, various planets, and the stars. It seemed obvious. We looked up, and everything passed by in orderly fashion above our heads. It was a system as elegant as it was predictable.

But a few of the details didn't quite fit. Celestial bodies didn't always show up in the night sky in the places where the model predicted. Greek and Roman astronomers had always assumed that was the result of gods warring in the heavens. But Copernicus believed there was only one God, and he had set up the heavens in an orderly fashion.

So, one day, merely as a thought experiment (a "mathematical fiction," he called it), he imagined what the universe might look like if something besides the earth stood at the center. What if, contrary to all appearances, the sun was at the center? He sketched out some rough diagrams. He guessed at a few of the calculations. His "fiction" fit the data better than the accepted Ptolemaic one.

Copernicus sent his findings to a publisher. The publisher reluctantly accepted the proposal, but before the book could be printed, Copernicus had a stroke and slipped into a coma. He awoke from the ensuing coma just long enough to look once at the finished book. Then he died.

The book, grippingly titled *De Revolutionibus Orbium Coelestium* ("On the Revolution of the Celestial Spheres"), was a cosmic flop. The publisher printed a mere four hundred copies of it and couldn't even sell them! Copernicus's revolution was a black hole of revenue, a supernova of red ink. He was widely panned as a fool "who wishes to turn the whole of astronomy upside down."[1]

But Copernicus's students believed their tutor had been onto something. They sifted through his notes and began writing their own books. And then, seemingly overnight, scientists changed their minds. The paradigm shift was so dramatic and so disorienting that historians labeled it the "Copernican Revolution."

As it turns out, it's a *good* thing the earth isn't the center of our solar system because it simply does not have the *gravitas* to keep all the other planets in orbit. Our sun does, and so it keeps all the planets, including ours, safely and securely in orbit.

Copernicus's revolution has an important corollary to our lives: Our lives don't work when we make ourselves the center of our own little universe either, even if God is one of our orbiting planets. We don't have the *gravitas* to keep it all together.

God didn't design us to be our own center. We aren't "big enough" to keep everything in orbit. Nor does it help to get religious, installing God as one of the spiritual bodies orbiting a life centered on us. That's why so many people—even though they are religiously busy—are joyless and unfulfilled. Even though God is a part of their lives, they still have something entirely too small at their center: themselves.

We need a spiritual revolution that is no less dramatic than Copernicus's astronomical revolution. We need *a Copernican Revolution of the soul.* As Gregory Koukl explains, it's not just that God has a plan for our lives; our lives exist for God's plan.[2]

This was another step I tried to skip in my faith. Even though I thought I had yielded fully to the authority of God, he wasn't at the center of my heart, mind, or understanding. So even after reading dozens of books defending the Christian faith, I was still groping around in a fog of fundamental questions.

I came closest to losing my faith while I served as a missionary to a Muslim community. I had learned to call many of these precious Muslims my friends. Even though I was doing what I believed God had commanded me to do, I struggled to understand the fairness and compassion of his ways. The same Bible that commanded me to love these people also said that they would perish apart from Christ. If God loved them, why wasn't he doing more to save them?

The more I thought about these things, the more questions I had. Why had God chosen such a seemingly inefficient way of getting the gospel to the nations? I know the usual response: "It's our fault—we just haven't obeyed Jesus's command to get the gospel to all nations." But why punish *them* for something *we* failed to do? Besides, God is God, so why not just employ another, more effective means? Why not send a fleet of angels on winged horses down to preach salvation in every city? Who is stopping him?

I remained at my post dutifully, doing what I was supposed to, but my heart teetered on the brink of unbelief. I didn't know the answers to these disturbing questions. I was scared there were no answers.

What I didn't realize was that my problems arose from having myself, instead of God, at the center of my universe.

THE REVOLUTIONARY TRUTH ABOUT THE CENTRALITY OF GOD'S GLORY

While I was on the mission field, I read a book by John Piper called *Desiring God*, which opened my eyes to a truth I had never understood before. This truth literally saved my faith. Although the book was not written specifically for the doubting, the central truth Piper puts forward pulled me back from unbelief: the pleasure of human beings is not the center of God's universe—God's glory is.[3]

"What?" you say. "God doesn't sit around all the time thinking about us? Isn't thinking about us all the time what it means for God to be love?" Yes and no. God is love, and Scripture tells us he never takes his loving eyes off us, but that is not the same as saying that we are the most important beings in the universe. God occupies the center of the universe because he is God. American Christian culture typically starts with the assumption that we are the most important beings in the universe, and our good and our glory is central to everything. Therefore, we conceive of God as the great, divine assistant—a supernatural butler—who comes into our lives to save us and help us find our best life now.

In all my years of reading Scripture, I'd failed to notice a theme that seems painfully obvious now: God's glory, not man's, is the underlying foundation of God's work.

Why did God create the earth? It brought him glory.

"The heavens declare the glory of God" (Ps 19:1).

Why did God choose to reveal salvation to and through the nation of Israel? It brought him glory.

"[God] saved them for his name's sake, to make his mighty power known" (Ps 106:8).

"For my name's sake I defer my anger; for the sake of my praise I restrain it for you.... For my own sake, for my own sake, I do it" (Isa 48:9, 11 ESV).

"Thus says the Lord GOD: It is not for your sake, O house

of Israel, that I am about to act, but for the sake of my
holy name ... and I will vindicate the holiness of my
great name ... and the nations will know that I am the
LORD" (Ezek 36:22–23 ESV).

Why did God choose to save us? It brought him glory.

"For he chose us in him before the creation of the world to
be holy and blameless in his sight ... to the praise of
his glorious grace" (Eph 1:4–6).

What does God want us doing with our lives now? Bringing him
glory.

"Whether you eat or drink or whatever you do, do it all for
the glory of God" (1 Cor 10:31).

We may be tempted to say, "Well, this all seems really petty of
God—like he loves himself more than he loves us." We don't like
people who think this way. Why would it be acceptable for God?

Brad Pitt and Oprah Winfrey both cite this among the primary
reasons they walked away from their faith. Oprah said she couldn't
accept the biblical teaching that God is "jealous" for our love. Brad
Pitt explained his dislike of Christianity by saying, "God says, 'You
have to say that I'm the best.' . . . It seemed to be about ego."[4] Even
C. S. Lewis, before becoming a Christian, was troubled by God's
focus on his glory. God's desire to be praised sounded to him, he
said, like "a vain woman who wants compliments."[5]

DOES GOD REALLY HAVE AN EGO PROBLEM?

Is God's insistence on being the center of it all rooted in an ego
problem? Before you give your final answer, consider this: If God
really is the source of all goodness and life, how would it be loving
for him to allow anything else to occupy the center?

Let's go back to Copernicus for a minute. The sun has to be the
center of the solar system in order for the planets to stay in orbit. It
would be unloving for the sun to allow the earth to be the center of

the solar system because doing so would lead to earth's destruction. It's just not big enough to be its own center.

In the same way, God's creation cannot thrive unless he—the source of goodness, love, and life—remains at the center. King David declared, "In your presence there is *fullness* of joy; at your right hand are pleasures *forevermore*" (Ps 16:11 ESV, emphasis mine). The most fulfilling, longest lasting joy comes from God. If God wants us to have that kind of joy, he will insist that he remains the center.

The reason it's wrong for anyone else to make themselves the center of their lives is simple: *they're not God.* That's the same reason it would be wrong and unloving for God to put anything else at the center too. As J. I. Packer says,

> If it is right for man to have the glory of God as his goal, can it be wrong for God to have the same goal? If man can have no higher purpose than God's glory, how can God? . . . The reason it cannot be right for man to live for himself as if he were God is because he is not God. However, it is not wrong for God to seek his own glory, because he is God.[6]

GOD'S COMMITMENT TO HIS GLORY IS GOOD NEWS FOR US

The best news of the Bible might be that the greatest way for God to bring glory to himself was by redeeming us. Jesus's sacrifice revealed a dimension of God's character that could not have been demonstrated in any other way. Through our salvation, God reveals his greatest glory.

A short biblical explanation of history reads like this:

> With the tip of his finger, God flung the skies, the galaxies, the oceans and the continents into existence, each declaring in its own way the wisdom and beauty of the Creator. In his final act, he made something special, something that would bring more glory to himself than all that had gone before it: a man and woman

made in his image. But he did something unusual before ending his work on his masterpiece. He handed this new man and woman the paintbrush and asked them to add the final stroke to creation, to paint in who they thought deserved to be at the center.[7]

Why would God do that? Because God knows what every person who has ever been in love knows—that love is only genuine when the person you love freely chooses to love you back. God wanted a creation held together by love, which meant giving his loved ones the ability to choose what they cherished.

We took the paintbrush, and instead of painting in God, we painted in *ourselves*. We said, "I think *I* should be at the center of this creation. After all, I've been around for nearly ten minutes." And every child ever since has been born into the world thinking about his or her needs rather than God's glory.

Two words no parent has ever had to teach their children are "no" and "mine." I didn't send my kids to "sin camp" to learn these words. They've never stayed after school to be tutored in selfishness. They didn't glean these things from their environment. When my youngest daughter was two, if she didn't want to eat what my wife and I gave to her, she'd look at us right in the face and dump her plate on the floor. She didn't learn that from watching us. I've never sat down for dinner and said to my wife, "You made meatloaf again?" and looked at her defiantly while I turned my plate upside down on the floor. My wife and I don't run around the house snatching the remote out of each other's hand screaming "mine!" and hitting each other on the head with it. Self-centeredness is an instinctive part of my children's nature.

Our default setting in life is self-centered, not God-centered. It's why when we look at a picture we're in, we have one method to determine whether the picture is good: how *we* look. It doesn't matter how everyone else looks. Your sister could have her eyes crossed, and your dad's toupee may be falling off, but as long as you look good, the picture is good. That's a pretty good metaphor for our lives: if things are going well for us, we believe we are having a good life.

Andy Stanley points out that even in our religious expression we reveal our self-centeredness. Most people's prayer lives could be summed up as *gimme, gimme, gimme.*

"God, make everyone behave the way I want them to behave so that I can be comfortable and happy."

"Pay him back for what he said to me."

"Work out this situation so it's easier for me."

And when God doesn't do it immediately, we become irate: "Hey God, what's wrong with you? Are you up there? Aren't you listening? Don't you get it? I'm talking. It's about me. What are you doing?" And, eventually, if God doesn't get on board, we threaten him with unbelief. That will show him! He won't get the pleasure of my faith and worship. He will learn.

But deep down we are genuinely confused. We say, "God, what could you possibly be up to?" And God says, "What am I up to? *Where have you been?* I'm 'up to' my glory."

It has always been about his glory. But from the beginning we hijacked his universe and made it about us.

So what was God supposed to do after his prized creation rebelled against his authority and stole his glory for themselves? Historically, governments have had a simple answer to questions like this: crush the rebels. Demonstrate their awesome power through great acts of strength. When first-century Jews dared to rebel against the Romans, the Roman army came down in force and hung thousands of Jewish rebels on crosses along the streets outside of Jerusalem. They tore down the walls of Israel's temple, demonstrating that nothing could stand in the way of their power.

What did the God of heaven do when his subjects rebelled against him?

> He made himself nothing
> by taking the very nature of a servant. (Phil 2:7)

He did what no earthly ruler has ever done, what you and I would never do. He humbled himself before the ones who had rebelled against him. He came as a servant. He washed their feet.

As Andy Stanley says it, he "refused to play the God-card." If I were God incarnate, I would play the God-card every chance I got. At a restaurant, I would demand, "Excuse me, could I get some service over here? . . . [*cough cough*]. I'm God." "Excuse me. I believe you're sitting in my seat. That's the God-chair."

But God didn't do that. He disguised his majesty, restrained his power, and went about the thankless task of rescuing us:

> He humbled himself
> by becoming obedient to death—
>   even death on a cross. (Phil 2:8)

Instead of crushing the traitors, he let *them* execute *him*. Did we appreciate it? No, we interpreted his sacrifice as weakness and spat in his face. We took his voluntary weakness as further validation that we were in charge.

But still, he wouldn't be deterred. He pursued those he loved all the way to the cross, where he bought back those who had betrayed and stolen from him.

Has any other ruler ever manifested his glory in such a way? We shoved God out of the picture, rebelled against his authority, and hijacked his creation. And God said, "I'll show *you* who deserves the glory!" And he mounted his warhorse and galloped across the universe . . . but as he got closer, he started laying aside his weapons of war and garments of glory. When he entered the world, he did so not as a mighty warrior but as a helpless baby.

> Therefore God exalted him to the highest place
>   and gave him the name that is above every name,
> that at the name of Jesus every knee should bow,
>   in heaven and on earth and under the earth,
> and every tongue acknowledge that Jesus Christ is Lord,
>   to the glory of God the Father. (Phil 2:9–11)

I love that word "therefore." Because Jesus did this, Paul says, we get an even *better* glimpse of God's glory. Through his humiliation and suffering, we see something about him that we couldn't have otherwise seen.

Maybe we missed his glory in creation. Maybe we managed to stay blind to it as we looked up through our telescopes into the majesty of the night sky or down through our microscopes into the glorious complexity of the human cell. But we can't miss it now! In God's great act of salvation, we saw that he was a God like no other, a God who did for his enemies what most of us wouldn't even do for our friends.

Can't you just hear Paul shouting that last sentence: *"Is not this God worthy of your love and worship? Will you not join in with the heavens in declaring his glory?"*

When you feel the weight of this glory, you won't need to be compelled to serve him. Or talk about him. You will *burn* to. You will cherish his glory because you would be lost without it.

King David got that. Isaiah too. So did Ezekiel, Paul, and Moses. Eventually, so did I.

Will you?

You will never understand your *purpose* in life until you see God's glory as the center of it all and its centrality as the greatest thing possible for humanity.

Everything on earth exists for *God's* glory. Hell exists because God's glorious perfection demands it. Jesus chose to suffer hell in our place so we could more clearly behold the glory of his mercy. He allows us to go through suffering because in suffering we can show people that he can give us joy in himself even when we are in great pain.

He chooses to use weak, fallible, redeemed humans to preach the gospel because that brings him more glory than sending an army of obligated angels to do the job. He has written human history so that its ultimate conclusion resounds for his glory. One day he will wipe away every tear and make us indescribably happy in him because that will bring him glory too.

If we submit to him, God's pursuit of his glory through us is the most enjoyable thing we could ever experience. If not, it will be the worst. God prefers to receive glory by demonstrating how happy he can make us in him. But if we reject that plan, he will get glory through us by showing how futile it is to oppose him.

Which aspect of glory we experience is up to us.

ONLY ONE CENTER

If you are going to follow the God who created it all, it's senseless to only go halfway. God won't fit well in the margins of your life. Christianity, it's been noted, makes for a terrible hobby. It's inconvenient, costly, and cumbersome. If you're going to walk with God, the only enjoyable way is to go all the way. Charles Spurgeon remarked that the most miserable person in the world is the half-committed Christian, just enough into God to be miserable in the world, but just enough into the world to be miserable in God.

My fear is that many of us have attempted to begin our faith journey without ever dealing with our *primary* problem: our usurpation of God's position at the center of our lives.

Maybe you're at a place in life where you've started to think about God again. You know something is missing; it's why you picked up this book. Maybe you're in a new life stage—like having kids—and you know that you need God as a part of your family. These are all good realizations, but I want to help you avoid a common mistake: making God *part* of your life rather than its center and source.

You cannot place the sun of God's glory into orbit in your life. It won't work. There's only one enjoyable way to walk with God: by abdicating your wrongful usurpation of him at the center and restoring him there.

Then, some of the most confusing parts of your life might start to make sense. Let me show you what I mean.

CHAPTER 14

HE WASN'T LATE
AFTER ALL

Robert E. Lee trusted few men more than Major General James Ewell Brown Stuart, or "Jeb" as he came to be known. Lee and Jeb had been friends for years before the Civil War began, serving together in the US Army in numerous military campaigns throughout the 1850s. Jeb was trustworthy, unflinchingly brave, and an expert in reconnaissance. Despite his peculiar flair for the dramatic (he would often lead his men into battles sporting a red cape, an ostrich plume, and drenched in cologne), Jeb was a serious soldier. General Lee said that Jeb was the only commander he trusted to bring him infallibly reliable intel. Lee called Jeb his "eyes."

Jeb literally ran circles around the Union's Army of the Potomac and reported every detail of their movement back to General Lee. Jeb's intel gave Lee the advantage at Second Bull Run, Fredericksburg, and Chancellorsville. By the summer of 1863, momentum in the war was swinging toward the Confederacy.

But in the moment Robert E. Lee needed him most, Jeb didn't show.

In June of 1863, Lee embarked on an audacious march north into the very heart of the Union. He ordered Jeb to parallel his march in the west, through the Shenandoah Valley. Instead, following a hunch, Jeb went *east*. He was attempting, against orders, to outflank the Union Army once again. But his decision left General Lee in the dark for eight days. During that time, Lee blindly stumbled across a group of soldiers in Gettysburg, Pennsylvania, who he assumed were a rag-tag local militia. Because Lee's "eyes" were off wandering miles away, Lee had no clue that he had just encountered the western tip of the primary Union army.

By the time Jeb's cavalry arrived in Gettysburg on July 2, he was too late. The battle of Gettysburg was nearly over. Furious, Lee called Jeb into his headquarters. All Lee could say was "General Stuart, where have you been?"

Had Jeb arrived when Lee expected him, historians say the battle of Gettysburg might have gone differently. Instead, Gettysburg marked the turning point in the war. General Lee must have asked himself again and again: "General Stuart, why were you late? Where were you?"

Where were you? It's a question we've all asked of somebody. Their absence or tardiness left us feeling abandoned, helpless, confused, and angry. If the stakes were high, we wondered if that person actually cared about us at all. Those moments when someone I depended on let me down have left me feeling helpless. When friends forget to call. When a trusted colleague doesn't deliver. When a teammate doesn't show up.

When the one who fails to show up as expected is God, it does more than disappoint. It can knock your faith off the rails.

"LORD, IF YOU HAD BEEN HERE . . ."

Mary and Martha felt this way about Jesus when their brother Lazarus got sick and died. Jesus, their friend, was not far away, and they had sent an urgent message for him to come straightaway.

"So when he heard that Lazarus was sick, he stayed where he was two more days" (John 11:6).

They waited. And waited. And Lazarus died. Then Jesus showed up. He offered no excuse.

Why hadn't he come? Didn't he love them? They thought he did. Everyone referred to Lazarus as the one Jesus loved (John 11:3). Did he not care after all?

Haven't you felt this way? These are the questions that almost every Christ-follower asks as they pass through a dark valley: Where are you, God? Why haven't you come? If you had been here . . . I wouldn't have failed. My parents wouldn't have gotten divorced. I wouldn't have gotten so hurt. My wife wouldn't have died.

I've asked it numerous times. In high school, I desperately wanted God to fix something in my heart. "God, why won't you resolve this for me? Why won't you just take care of this so I can move on?" In college, I asked God to take away all my doubts. "God, surely you want me to believe with confidence. If you exist, I want to know for sure. I know that you could take away all my doubts in an instant. Why won't you do that?" *Why are you not showing up when I need you?*

Jesus's tardiness in coming to Lazarus was not due to a lack of care. As Jesus would explain, God had orchestrated this situation for a greater purpose—to reveal his glory through his control and ultimate victory over all things (John 11:4).

I'll go ahead and give you the punchline: Jesus raises Lazarus from the dead. But along the way, Jesus teaches us what faith in a really big and sometimes confusing God looks like.

Jesus was doing three things in Mary's and Martha's pain, and they are what he's doing in your pain as well.

HE'S WEEPING

When Jesus hears firsthand from Mary that Lazarus had died, he weeps (John 11:35). Jesus's tears have always struck me as a little strange. Didn't he know he was about to raise Lazarus from the dead? If you know that in less than ten minutes a loved one will be alive, why cry? Instead, why not say to Mary and Martha, "No, no! You don't need to cry! I'm about to fix everything!"

I am a big college basketball fan, and sometimes games I want to watch happen during our services, so I record them to watch later. Invariably, someone spoils the outcome for me before I get home. If I find out that my team has won, I'm still excited to watch the game because even when something bad happens, I can say, "Who cares? In the end we win." The bad calls, which normally drive me insane, don't bother me that much. So why would Jesus weep knowing that in just a few minutes he was about to fix everything? It makes no sense.

But then I had kids, and I realized what it's like to see someone you really love go through pain, even when you know the pain is temporary. When your heart is closely knit together with someone else's, their pain causes you pain.

It's true that one day God will wipe away every tear and make every sad thing come untrue. To God, that moment seems like it is only seconds away (2 Pet 3:8)! Even so, when we are in pain now, he feels it. He has united his heart with ours. So when our heart is broken, his is too. When we weep, he weeps.

I know that Jesus will one day raise the dead, and I know he will take the worst situations and use them for his glory and my good. But when I'm hurting, maybe the most comforting truth of all is knowing that Jesus weeps with me.

He's not late because he doesn't care. He's late because he's up to something greater.

HE'S SAVING

When Jesus first heard about Lazarus's sickness, he emphatically declared that this bout of death would not have the final word.

"But when Jesus heard it he said, 'This illness does not lead to death'" (John 11:4 ESV). But Lazarus did die! Jesus was looking past Lazarus's death to his resurrection. This sickness did not lead *to* death; it led *through* death to a resurrection. Death was just a brief stop along the way.

When Martha, Lazarus's other sister, told Jesus about her brother's death, Jesus responded by saying, "Your brother will rise again" (John 11:23). To be frank, Jesus's words here seem a little bit insensitive. If I were mentoring a pastor on how to do hospital visits, and this was the first thing he said to the weeping family after someone died, I'd tell him to work on his bedside manner. Imagine a funeral of a wife who tragically lost her husband. You wouldn't slap her on the back and say, "What are you crying for? Haven't you read the *Left Behind* books? It's called the rapture, sister. Have some faith."

Jesus wasn't just offering her a theology lesson about the future. He was attempting to change her perspective on the present. We are to live in present awareness of eternal life. Martha didn't see that at first, so she responded with a good Sunday school answer, saying, "I know that he will rise again in the resurrection on the last day" (John 11:24). She knew her theology.

Jesus says, *But I'm talking about more than resurrection on the last day . . .*

> I am the resurrection and the life. Whoever believes in me, though he die, yet shall he live, and everyone who lives and believes in me shall never die. Do you believe this? (John 11:25–26)

I am the resurrection and the life *right now*. In other words, I'm already turning the power of death around, using its powers of destruction to glorify my name and heal you. In me, even when you die, you don't *really* die.

To her credit, Martha believes. I suspect that many people in the church today don't. We still act like our "illness" terminates in death. What scares us about death is that it feels like permanent loss. Someone we loved is gone *forever*. But Jesus took all these permanent, bitter parts of death into himself so that none of it remains for us. As Paul explained, Jesus takes away death's sting (1 Cor 15:55).

A dad was driving down the highway with his little girl when a yellow-jacket flew in through the window. As I've done many times, he tried to shoo it out the window without dying in a fiery car wreck. But he couldn't get it out. It began to hover around his little girl, who was terribly allergic to beestings. She called out, "Daddy, Daddy! It's going to sting me!"

The dad pulled the car over to the side of the road and hopped into the back. Still unable to get the bee out, he cornered the bee against the windshield with his hand. He then closed his hand around the bee and braced himself for the inevitable sting. After it stung him, he opened his hand outside the car and released the bee.

The little girl began panicking again, "Daddy, it's going to come back!" The father opened his hand, showing her the stinger embedded in his hand, and said to the little girl, "No, sweetheart, don't worry about that bee. It can't hurt you anymore."

Jesus took the sting of death into his hands so that in him we have nothing more to fear. Death, the mighty enemy, has been reduced to a temporary, inconvenient nuisance.

As Jesus walked up to Lazarus's grave, the apostle John tells us he was "deeply moved" (John 11:38), a Greek phrase indicating not just sadness, but anger—the kind of anger you might feel at someone who has hurt or threatened someone you love. Some scholars say you can translate that word "snorted," like a bull about to charge into battle. And then, like a fighter, Jesus yells out in a loud voice, "Lazarus, come out!" (11:43).

Lazarus, who had now been dead for four days, comes staggering out of the grave. By the way, "four days" was significant to Jews because they believed that a person's spirit hovered above their dead body for three days to see if some miracle might rejoin the soul to the body. By the fourth day Jews believed the spirit had given up hope and gone on to heaven. Death at four days was considered irreversible.

Not for Jesus. In him death was finished, and after his resurrection there remains no power that can ever threaten his people. That's because in dying for his people he took death's terrible sting.

At the grave of Lazarus, we get a glimpse into both *how* God feels and *what* he is doing in the life of each one of his children. First, we know that whatever the reason for our suffering, it's not because he lacks love for us. At the cross, we see that he loved us so intensely that he not only wept over our pain, he took the sting of our penalties of sin on himself. Second, in his resurrection we see that he has reversed death itself, not only removing its power but undoing its effects. We see that in the end he will be glorified and our knowledge of him will be deepened.

This leads to one final insight we glean from this encounter about what God is doing when we're suffering and don't know why.

HE'S GLORIFYING

Jesus told his disciples that the biggest objective he was pursuing in this encounter was God's glory.

As we saw in the previous chapter, through every episode of our pain God is writing a story for his glory. Like Mary and Martha, we sometimes can't see where that story is going, how our pain fits into it, or why Jesus seems to arrive too late to help us. But because of stories like this one, we can rest assured that he is always working.

I've heard God's work in our lives compared to the weaving of a tapestry. On one side you see a beautiful, intricate work of art. But if you lift the corner and look on the backside, you find an erratic and chaotic mess of strands. If all you could see were the backside of a tapestry as it was being woven, you would conclude that nothing beautiful was taking shape. When you flip it and look at it from the front, however, you see that every strand finds its perfect place according to the plan of the artist. One day, God will "flip over" history, and we will see that every strand of our lives was part of a picture God wove together for his glory.

Part of that beauty is something he is weaving *into* us. Through suffering we come to know him better. He breaks up our confidence in ourselves. We develop compassion for others. We understand how much better God is than all earthly gifts, how he alone has power over death, and how he is faithful to sustain us even in pain. Through our pain, we experience parts of God we may not otherwise know! These are not easy or cheap lessons. They are costly and often brutal. But they are beautiful.

In 1 Corinthians, Paul says that one day "death will be swallowed up in victory." When you swallow something, it becomes part of you. Paul doesn't say that the memory of death will simply vanish. It becomes *part* of us, making us better for having gone through it. Death itself contributes to God's beautiful picture.

There was an ancient tribe in Japan renowned for its pottery. After creating magnificent, beautifully painted vessels, they would smash them against a rock. Then they would fasten the hundreds of pieces back together with melted gold sealing the seams. The restored pottery was infinitely more valuable than it was before it had been broken.

God is doing the same thing with us. He allows life to smash us sometimes so that he can fill the broken places in our lives with himself. One day, our union with Christ will be our greatest source of joy. We will literally be in him, and he in us—one with him, remade in his likeness forever. The bitterness of death will be forgotten, and we will be richer and more beautiful for having gone through the process.

I still look back on some of the most painful chapters in my life—moments I couldn't understand why God wasn't doing what I *begged* him to do, moments it seemed obvious what needed to be done. But *already* I can see some of the good things God was bringing out of those moments. He was sharpening my vision. He was rooting out idols and breaking up faulty foundations, revealing areas of blindness and unbelief, and teaching me to be more compassionate. I can already see how he has poured his "gold" into many of the broken cracks of my life. I am confident that in eternity, I'll see how he was doing that through all my painful moments.

IT'S GOD'S STORY, NOT OURS

Never forget: the story isn't about you. Knowing that enables you to experience a new kind of joy in the journey.

As Jesus told his disciples, this was ultimately a story about *God's* glory, not Lazarus's healing. Mary, Martha, and Lazarus couldn't see it yet, but God was using this situation to teach *other* people—people they had never met—about his glory. The forty-four verses that tell their story were agonizing to go through. But here we are, two thousand years later, still talking about them.

John tells us, "Many of the Jews therefore who had come with Mary, and had seen what Jesus did, believed in him" (John 11:45). In the same way, through our pain, others see the value of God's promises. Sometimes they get to see God's miraculous power to heal. Other times they get to see that God's presence is better to us than healing. Sometimes they get a glimpse of Jesus's grace through our willingness to forgive.

Are you willing to undergo that kind of pain if it helps others come to know God?

A friend of mine did something in his church called "cardboard testimonies," where members wrote a phrase on one side of a piece of cardboard that encapsulated their lives before Christ, and then flipped it over to reveal a phrase expressing the difference Christ made in their lives. People came up to the front in succession and revealed their cards. During the presentation, a woman and man walked on stage together. The front of her card said, "Diagnosed with MS." His said, "Doctor who diagnosed the disease. An atheist." He flipped his over, and it said, "Through her testimony, baptized last month." Then she flipped hers over, and it said, "Worth it."

Are you willing for your story to be a strand of God's glory woven into someone else? Can you say, "Worth it"?

Nothing is more liberating than embracing that the events of your life are not primarily about you, that God is the main character in this story, and that the pursuit of his glory is history's driving theme.

Every movie has major characters and minor ones. What happens to minor characters is less important. Minor characters exist to serve the storyline of the main character.

For example, you probably don't know the name "Biggs Darklighter" (unless you're a nerd like me). But you probably know the name "Luke Skywalker." Yet if it weren't for Biggs Darklighter, Luke's story would have stopped before it started.

Biggs Darklighter was "Red Three," the X-wing fighter pilot who thrust his spacecraft between Luke's fighter and the Imperial TIE fighter trying to destroy him. The lasers intended for Luke went into Biggs's ship. Biggs died, and Luke lived. Biggs's role in the movie lasted only ninety seconds and most people don't even know his name. But his story is an important part of the whole.

How would you like to be Biggs Darklighter? You spent all this time preparing to be an X-wing fighter. X-wing school was very difficult to get into, but you did it. You studied, mastered the art of flying, acted with bravery, and no one even knows your name. You were only in the story to serve the purpose of the bigger story—the story of Luke Skywalker and the new hope he brought.

Coming to Jesus is like stepping out of a movie where you were the main character into one where you are just a minor character. What happens to *you* becomes less important than how your story serves the more important story. When you prosper, you ask, "How should my prosperity be used to extend *his* story?" When you go through pain, you ask, "How can my pain better tell his story?" And when no one gives you credit for your sacrifice, you aren't devastated because his story rolls on.

You know that when the credits roll at the end, and the audience rises to their feet in applause, you get to have a part in the celebration. And with Jesus, the cheers go on forever.

HE COULD HAVE STOPPED THE COMMUNISTS

John and Betty Stam walked away from the potential for a lucrative medical career in the United States to serve as missionary doctors to China. The 1930s were not a good time to be in China, especially for foreigners, as this was the beginning of the bloody and brutal Communist revolution.

On the afternoon of December 8, 1934, word came to Betty, while she was in her home with her newborn baby girl, that the Communists were approaching their village of Miaoshou. When Mao Zedong's Red Army conquered a new village, they routinely executed the foreigners.

Betty knew there was no chance she and John could escape, and she knew that the Communists would either kill her baby outright or abandon her to die. So in the five minutes she had before the Communist soldiers stormed into her home, she wrapped their baby girl tightly in a blanket with some money pinned on it for whoever found her. She then hid her baby in a closet, seconds before the Communists arrived.

The Communists marched Betty and John up a hill outside the village and shot them, along with many of the other villagers. Their infant daughter lay alone in the closet for more than two days. The village had been completely evacuated, and no one even knew she was there.

A couple days later, a Chinese believer was passing through the village, and remarkably he heard the baby's cries from the closet.

Chinese believers took in newborn Helen Priscilla Stam and raised her until she was five, after which they sent her back to the United States to live with relatives.

One of the Stams' friends later remarked that if God was sovereign enough to miraculously direct one of the few believers in China to baby Helen's hiding place in the closet, was he not also sovereign enough to save John and Betty if he wanted?[1]

If so, why didn't he?

I know it would make a beautiful story if I could answer that question. As in, if I could tell you that the guard who shot John and Betty saw their love and courage in their dying moments, realized the futility of Communism, and went on to become one of China's greatest evangelists.

But a lot of the time we don't know the reason why things happen or what God is doing through them.

It's like John Piper says, at any given moment God is doing about ten thousand different things in your life, and you are probably aware of only three of them.[2]

When he doesn't do something the way we think he should, it's not because he has ceased to care. Small providences, like Helen's preservation and Lazarus's resurrection, show us that God is in control and that he never lays down his pen in the story he's writing. He's always working.

We have more than mere small providences to show us that. We have Jesus's willful journey to the cross and his all-conquering resurrection.

Not one thread in our lives is out of place. Jesus is never absent, never forgetful, and never late.

DO YOU TRUST HIM?

Do you trust in a God big enough to direct everything in your life to his glorious, joy-filled end? Can you trust him even when you are not sure how a particular thread contributes to the beautiful picture he is weaving in history's tapestry?

His "tardiness" is just an illusion. When we get to heaven, we'll see, like Mary, Martha, and Lazarus, that Jesus wasn't late after all.

Trust in God's character, not understanding his ways, is the faith that overcomes the world. It's the faith that not only gives you hope in the midst of trials but compels you to tell others about a truth that goes deeper than death.

When you are convinced of the loving sovereignty of Jesus, you'll discover you just have to tell others about him. Your burning heart will soon seek for itself a flaming tongue.

CHAPTER 15

BURNING HEARTS, FLAMING TONGUES

Rhonda, a girl in her midtwenties, grew up in New England and was about as unfamiliar with the Christian message as any American I'd ever met. So I started with the basics—who God is and why Jesus came. She asked a lot of questions. But I wasn't prepared for the question she asked toward the end:

"You *actually* believe this?"

"Yes, of course I do," I said.

She replied, "Because if I *actually* believed what you are saying—that everyone in my life who didn't know Jesus was separated from God's love and headed to hell—I'm not sure how I would make it through the day. I would constantly be on my knees pleading with people to listen. But you . . . you don't seem *that* bothered by all this. You are a great debater, but you don't seem that upset that I am not persuaded."

I didn't know what to say. I knew she was right. I was *saying* all the right things, but my heart did not reflect the gravity of what I was saying.

I've come to see this as a form of unbelief—assenting to truths with our mind while hardening our heart to their realities. How does a person who *really* believes the gospel feel about the world?

Charles Spurgeon was once asked by one of his students whether those who had never heard about Jesus could ever be saved. "A troubling question indeed," he consented. But even more troubling, he said, was whether we who know the gospel and do nothing to bring it to the lost could actually be saved. He said,

> If Jesus is precious to you, you will not be able to keep your good news to yourself. You will be whispering it into your child's ear; you will be telling it to your husband; you will be earnestly imparting it to your friend; without the charms of eloquence you will be more than eloquent; your heart will speak, and your eyes will flash as you talk of his sweet love. . . . Every Christian here is either a missionary or an impostor.[1]

Burning hearts, he went on to say, will always result in flaming tongues. Anyone who really encounters Jesus won't need to be compelled to talk about him. They won't be able to stay silent.

This is exactly what we hear when Paul explains to the Corinthians why he is willing to go to such extreme measures to get the gospel to others: "Christ's love compels us, because we are convinced that one died for all, and therefore all died. And he died for all, that those who live should no longer live for themselves but for him who died for them and was raised again" (2 Cor 5:14–15). This love of Christ is both love *for* Christ and a sense of *his* love for sinners, both of which will burn in our hearts.

BURNING WITH LOVE FOR CHRIST

When we love something, we enjoy talking about it. In *Reflections on the Psalms*, C. S. Lewis says, "We delight to praise what we enjoy because the praise not merely expresses but completes the enjoyment; it is its appointed consummation."[2]

Think about how much you enjoy talking about your favorite TV series—that one you binge-watched for two days straight. Or your grandkids. Or how much people who do CrossFit enjoy talking about their routines: "Yeah, this morning we did a hundred burpees and thirty-five goblet squats; I balanced a 757 tire on my head and carried Phil from accounting for three hundred yards."

In each of these cases, it's not a sense of obligation that moves us to talk about these things. It's delight. We'd be pained *not* to talk about them.

This, Lewis says, is the essence of worship. Delight in the heart that produces praise on the tongue.

> It is not out of compliment that lovers keep on telling one another how beautiful they are; the delight is incomplete till it is expressed. It is frustrating to have discovered a new author and not to be able to tell anyone how good he is; to come suddenly, at the turn of the road, upon some mountain valley of unexpected grandeur and then to have to keep silent because the people with you care for it no more than for a tin can in the ditch; to hear a good joke and find no one to share it with.[3]

When we genuinely love God, we want others to know him too. In a city not far from where I lived in Southeast Asia, each year a group of Hindus engaged in a sacred ritual to wash away their sins. They attached sleds to their bare backs by inserting the hooks connected to ropes through their skin. They then drag the sled down the street toward the Hindu temple. Blood flows from their wounds and speckles the streets as they pass. Upon arriving at the temple, they wash their cuts in sacred waters, believing that this process washes away their sins.

How can those of us who know the gospel not burn to tell them that Jesus paid it all, that "sin had left a crimson stain, he washed it white as snow"?[4]

Do we *really* believe the gospel? Has its truth set our hearts ablaze? Can we really believe and not care?

Are we missionaries or are we imposters?

COMPASSION: FILLED WITH THE LOVE OF CHRIST

If we really believe the gospel, simple compassion compels us to share it. How could we do otherwise?

Sometimes we talk about evangelism in the strangest ways—as if, for example, we need to wait until we're "prompted" by the Holy Spirit to share with someone. But imagine you're walking through a big city downtown when you see a little boy lying on the railroad tracks, alive but unconscious. In the distance, you hear a train coming. Do you need to stop and pray about what God wants you to do? You don't review your list of priorities, your Myers-Briggs personality profile, or your spiritual gifts matrix to ask if this is really God's plan for you. Simple compassion compels you to pick up the little boy and move him to safety.

What kind of response is required by the knowledge that over 2.2 billion people in the world have little to no access to the gospel?

When you hear that kind of number, try not to reduce it to a statistic. Each of those represents a *person*.

Josef Stalin is reported to have said, "The death of one is a tragedy; the death of a million is just a statistic." That's a chilling statement coming from him. What he meant was that when we are confronted with the face of one, we see in that person someone just like us. When we think of people as numbers, we forget that each one is an individual.

Each of those 2.2 billion people are made in the image of God just like you and me, and they experience pain, loneliness, fear, and sadness just like us. Going to hell is every bit the tragedy for them that it would be for us or one of our children. The 2.2 billion aren't a demographic measurement. They are people.

So are the one in seven people in the world classified as "desperately poor," and the nearly 100,000 children who die each day of starvation and poverty-related diseases. So are the 150 million children living as orphans. Each of them woke up this morning just like one of my children, only with no father or mother to look after them. So are the 30 million people who live in slavery, mostly young girls, 80 percent of whom are trafficked for sex. So are the 60 million people in our world who live as refugees, displaced from their homes by war or tragedy.

Behind every single one of those numbers is a name, a face, a soul. At some point, each one had the same heart full of excitement and hope about the future that you had when you were a child.

Thinking about the lostness of the world can be overwhelming. I know I can't save the world, but I have to do *something*.

For a long time, I hardened myself against those statistics because I thought, "It's not fair. God's not fair. If he really cared, he would do something." I refused to embrace what my Bible said, as if putting my head in the sand would change the reality. But as I began to humble myself under the awesome authority of God, submitting myself to his will, and conceding that his ways are indeed just, true, and good even when I can't understand them, I began to see that what was actually unfair was that I had experienced the grace of Jesus and was *not doing anything about it.*

I am not in a place to cast judgment on the ways of God. What I am responsible for, however, is his revelation that he desires all people to come to repentance and that the only way they will hear about it is through me (2 Pet 3:9; Rom 10:14–17). I literally *owe* the gospel to others.

GOD, WILL YOU LET ME GO?

The first time I really wrestled with this was when I was a junior in college. I had become a Christian just four years before and thought

I could serve God best as a lawyer. By my junior year of college, my pre-law courses were going well, and my path forward seemed clear. But during that spring semester, at the urging of my pastor, I read through the book of Romans seven times.

One Friday morning, on my sixth or seventh trip through the book, I came to Romans 2:12, which seemed to lift off the page: "For all who have sinned without the law will also perish without the law, and all who have sinned under the law will be judged by the law" (ESV).

Those who haven't heard of Jesus, Paul says, are still under the judgment of God because they have a law written on their hearts. Each of us is without exception, having rebelled against this inward law and suppressed the truth about God written on our consciences. Our only hope, Paul concludes, is the undeserved second chance of the gospel (Rom 10:14–17).

This explains why Paul begins the book of Romans by calling himself a debtor to both the Jew and the Greek, under obligation to bring the gospel to them whatever the cost (Rom 1:14–16). The word for "debtor" is the same one you would use if somebody owed you a large sum of money. But Paul had never even met those Greeks and Romans. What could he possibly owe them?

Jesus had done something for Paul that placed him in debt. Paul knew that he was no worthier of the gospel than the Greeks and Romans, and that with this undeserved kindness came the obligation to take it to those who had yet to hear it.

This meant Paul was not a free man, so to speak. When you are a financial debtor, you are no longer free to use your resources however you like. If you owe American Express $498,212.38, then you are not free to spend any excess income as you wish. American Express has a claim on it. Your tax refund of $618.64 will not go toward a larger television. It will go to American Express. That's the life of a debtor.

We who have been saved by extravagant grace are not free

to spend our lives however we please. We *owe* the lost the gospel, and we only have one lifetime to fulfill our obligation to them. The unreached literally have a *claim* on our lives. David Platt, president of the International Mission Board, says, "Every saved person this side of heaven owes the gospel to every unsaved person this side of hell." The greatest injustice in the church occurs when those of us who know the gospel not to do all we can to get it to those who don't.

As I sat in my dorm room that morning, this truth took on a personal dimension for me. I sat in stunned silence for several minutes. Prior to this moment, I had been open to God calling me into ministry, but I assumed if he wanted that he would show me through some dramatic "Damascus Road" experience. He would appear to me in a dream and tell me to go to Papua, New Guinea, or spell out "take the gospel to Indonesia" in my Cheerios. But nothing like that had ever happened. No bright lights. No voices. No cryptic messages in my Cheerios.

But that morning, in light of what I now knew about the gospel, everything felt different. It was as if for the past four years I had been asking God the wrong question. So I changed my question to "God, will you let me go and tell them? Please God, I want to go. If you let me go, I will go. Here I am; send me." I then sensed the Holy Spirit say, "You may go." I felt like for the first time in my Christian life I was praying the right prayer.

We shouldn't have to be "called" to engage in the Great Commission. The call to leverage our lives for the Great Commission was included in the gift of salvation. The question is no longer *if* you are called, only *where* and *how*. We are obligated by an inner gratitude for the gospel to look at whatever gifts and opportunities God has placed in our hands and ask how they can best be used to bring salvation to others.

I was sitting around trying to "find the will of God," but it had never been lost! God says he's unwilling that any should perish (2 Pet 3:9). His will for the lost helps me understand his will for my life.

There's nothing wrong with a career in law, politics, teaching, sports, or business. God gifts many believers for these fields. The point is that any experience of grace brings with it the sacred responsibility to *share* that experience. I've heard it said that our God is like a spiritual tornado. He never draws you in without hurling you back out! You must consider how your profession can be leveraged for the mission.

Where God sends you is up to him, but *whether* he has called you is settled.

As I sat in my dorm room that morning, overwhelmed by the crushing lostness of the world, I realized I had only three options:

I could deny the truth of the gospel. To be honest, that's what I wanted to do—to widen the gate to eternal life and pretend that Jesus hadn't really said he was the *only* way, the truth, and the life. I wanted to deny that hell exists. But I knew I couldn't do that, unless I was prepared to walk away from the faith altogether. I knew that intellectual integrity requires that we either acknowledge Jesus as Lord or we don't. Either I believed Jesus had been sent by God to reveal the truth, or it was time to walk away. And I knew I couldn't walk away.

I could ignore these truths. I could put my head in the sand and live as if they weren't true. This seems to be what most North American Christians do—to act like church is primarily about adding harmony and balance to their lives, providing their kids with a moral code, and enabling them to live a happy and fulfilled life. But I knew that option was just as bad, if not worse, than outright unbelief. At least if you denied the faith, you weren't a hypocrite. Saying that you believe that heaven and hell are real and doing nothing about it seems to be hypocrisy of the highest order.

I could embrace the truth and live accordingly. I could recognize that God, in grace, had revealed the truth about Jesus to me just like he had to Paul—not because I was worthier than others, but because God intended to use me also as a vessel to carry that message to others. I could embrace that the privilege of hearing the gospel came with the responsibility of spreading it. I could simply respond, "Here I am, Lord. Send me." That's what I did.

COMPELLED BY LOVE

Do the attitudes of your heart line up with what you confess with your mouth? In the book of Romans, the apostle Paul tells us that the implications of the gospel were so weighty to him that "I have great sorrow and unceasing anguish in my heart. For I could wish that I myself were cursed and cut off from Christ for the sake of my people, those of my own race, the people of Israel" (Rom 9:2–4). Think about this: Paul was willing to be "cut off from Christ"—that is, to personally *go to hell*—if that meant that Israel, his beloved country, would find salvation. We might be tempted to write that off as a rhetorical flourish, except that Paul insists three times that it's not: "*I speak the truth in Christ—I am not lying, my conscience confirms it through the Holy Spirit*" (Rom 9:1). Paul normally didn't feel the need to bolster his statements with reassurances that he was actually telling the truth. But in this case, he wants us to know he is not exaggerating. His heart is so broken over the lostness of Israel that he would, if he could, go to hell in their place!

Has God's love given you this kind of yearning to see others saved?

Evangelism can be difficult, but at its core it's quite simple. It's not about knowing the complexities of theology or about having all the answers. It's about understanding that Jesus saved you from judgment by paying your sin-debt and sharing that news with others. It's about understanding that the incredible love Christ has for you, he also has for others.

We simply cannot experience the magnitude of salvation and remain silent. Embracing the awesomeness of the gospel ignites a burning heart, and a burning heart leads to a flaming tongue. Every time.

Shortly after my experience that morning in the book of Romans, I encountered a letter that Adoniram Judson, one of the first American Baptist missionaries, wrote to his prospective father-in-law asking for his daughter Ann Hasseltine's hand in marriage. It crushed me. Judson wrote,

> I have now to ask whether you can consent to part with your daughter early next spring, to see her no more in this world. . . . Whether you can consent to her departure to (foreign, dangerous) lands, and her subjection to the hardships and sufferings of a missionary life? Whether you can consent to her exposure to . . . every kind of want and distress; to degradation, insult, persecution, and perhaps a violent death? Can you consent to all this, for the sake of him who left his heavenly home and died for her and for you; for the sake of perishing, immortal souls; for the sake of Zion and the glory of God? Can you consent to all this, in hope of soon meeting your daughter in the world of glory, with a crown of righteousness brightened by the acclamations of praise which shall redound to her Savior from (lost nations) saved, through her means, from eternal woe and despair?[5]

How would you like to get a letter like that from a guy dating your daughter?

Unfortunately, Judson's life unfolded much as he anticipated. He and Ann lost their first three children to disease in Burma, and Ann spent long periods alone as he languished in a Burmese prison. She died of smallpox in her early thirties.

Judson recognized the possibility that all this might happen. He and Ann evaluated the cost together and said it's worth it "for the sake of perishing, immortal souls, for the sake of Zion (i.e., the kingdom of Jesus) and the glory of God."

This is the privilege—and sacred responsibility—to which we are called. We are not guaranteed safety. We are guaranteed Jesus. And he is enough.

What he did for us, we are to do for others. Ask yourself: Where would you be without Jesus? The same place millions of people in the world—and probably some in your neighborhood—are without you. Jesus's death does someone no good until they hear about it (Rom 10:14–17).

I can't talk about these things without thinking about the last conversation I had before leaving Southeast Asia, where I lived for two years in a Muslim village. Just a few hours before I left, Ahmed, a man who had become one of my closest friends, came to visit me. Ahmed was as committed a Muslim as I'd ever met. He knew the ins and outs of his religion, practiced them studiously, and was gracious and kind. He even volunteered his afternoons to serve underprivileged Islamic youth.

Whenever I would talk about Jesus, he would smile and say, "You, my friend, are a good man of faith. You were born in a Christian country, and you honor the faith of your parents. I was born in a Muslim country, and I honor the faith of mine. You were born a Christian and will die a Christian. I was born a Muslim, and I will die a Muslim. That is how it will always be."

The week before I was scheduled to leave, I'd tried to talk to Ahmed about Jesus one last time. I told him that, according to the Bible, only Jesus can save us. For about fifteen minutes, he sat politely and listened as I poured out my heart. When I finished, he thanked me again for my friendship and left. I did not see him again until my last day. When he showed up, I could tell something was troubling him, so I asked him what it was.

"Our conversation," he said. "After we talked the other day, I thought about how much I appreciated you for telling me so directly what you believed. But then I dismissed it like I always do." He paused. "Or at least I tried to. Last night as I was trying to go to sleep I couldn't stop thinking about it. Then, when I feel asleep, I had a dream—if it's even right to call it that."

He paused again to gather his thoughts and continued. "At

first, I thought it was one of those dreams that comes from eating strange fish. But I've had many of those kinds of dreams. This was something different. This was a dream from Allah.

"I was standing on earth when suddenly, open before my feet, was the 'straight and narrow way' leading to heaven. As I looked up along this pathway to heaven, *you* were on it!" (He seemed so surprised by this that I felt a little offended.)

"You arrived at heaven's gates, but the way inside was blocked by huge, brass doors. I thought to myself, 'This is where his journey ends. Who has the power to open those doors?'

"But then, as I watched, someone from inside knew you and called your name. The doors then swung open wide for you, and you went in . . . and my heart broke because I really wanted to go with you. But then the doors opened again, and you came back out, walked back down the path a little way, and stretched your hand out to me down here on earth. Then you pulled me up to heaven with you."

He then looked at me and said, "What do you think my dream means?"

Now, please understand that I was raised in a traditional, Baptist home. Dreams were not a part of our standard religious repertoire. But in that moment, I knew what to say: "Brother, you are in luck. Dream interpretation is my spiritual gift!"

We talked for a half hour about how he could be saved. I would love to tell you that he became a Christian. He did not. But it is what he said next that will probably haunt me forever: "I know what my dream means, J. D. You were sent here by God to help me find the way of salvation. But tonight, you are going back to America, and you are *the only Christian I have ever known.* Who now will help me find the way?"

All over the world, all over this country, and all over *your* neighborhood, people like Ahmed are asking that question.

Evangelism is not a task that you put on a spiritual to-do list.

Evangelism is the overflow of genuine belief in the gospel. When you grasp the magnitude of God's grace toward you and the lostness of the world, there is only one possible response: *Here I am, Lord. Send me.*

And when that is your prayer, you'll feel something more than passion stirring in your heart—you'll sense a divine energy at your back. Heaven stands ready to assist you.

CHAPTER 16

HEAVEN AT YOUR BACK

Last Sunday, I found myself face to face with a group of convicted felons. Actually, that happens every Sunday. A group of prisoners nearing the end of their sentences participate in a program that allows them to gradually reenter society by interacting with host families from our church. Many attend church with these families each weekend. They sit together in the front section, so we are face to face at least once a week.

Many of these men have been incarcerated for more than a decade. One told me recently that he had always assumed the months leading up to his release would be filled with excitement. Instead, he said, he felt an emotion he wasn't expecting: *fear.* Did he still have what it takes to survive in the real world? Had he ever? He had made a mess of his life the first time. Would he do it again?

Everyone feels insecure at some point, especially on the eve of a big change. Insecurity is that voice inside that whispers, "I can't succeed at this because I am not _____ enough." For example,

- You just got hired for a new job, and nobody else seems to think you can do it. Every time a group gathers at the water cooler, you're pretty sure they are talking about you.
- You're dating someone and unsure if you measure up to their

family's expectations. Dinners with the parents feel like a
job interview. You're pretty sure that at the next family tribal
council you are going to get voted off the island.

- You've just entered some new phase of life, such as college,
newfound independence, or retirement, and you're not sure
you have what it takes to succeed.

- You're a new parent. Parenting is one of those things that the
more you do it, the less competent you feel at it. Before I had
kids, I had four—count them—solid theories on parenting. And
I taught them to everyone. I think I even published a couple.
Now I have four kids and *no* great theories on parenting.

- God has called you to a ministry and you feel utterly
incapable for it.

- He's put on your heart to share Christ with someone, but you
just don't think you can do it.

In the age of Periscope and Instagram, our feelings of insecurity
are exacerbated by instant comparison. No matter what we do, we
can always find someone out there doing it better. A friend of mine
says he never goes on Instagram around Valentine's Day because it
makes whatever he has done for his wife seem pitiful. He wrote his
wife a poem and took her to her favorite restaurant. Not bad, until
he learned about the guy who got his girl a pony and took her back-
packing through Europe. Thanks a lot @CleverTrevor42.

What goes into your "I am not _____ enough" blank most
often? Do you not feel smart enough? Attractive enough? Young
enough? Spiritual enough?

When God found Moses, he had tons of words to fill in that blank.

FORTY YEARS OF FAILURE

Moses felt like a complete failure. He had once dreamed of rescuing
his countrymen from slavery in Egypt, but his first attempt ended

in disaster. The Israelites rejected him, he killed a policeman, and Pharaoh put a death sentence on his head. That's one awful day at work: everyone hates you, your boss fires you, and you kill someone on the way out to the parking lot.

For forty years, Moses wandered around the desert nursing that failure. So when God appeared to Moses in his eighties with the command to reconfront Pharaoh, Moses stuttered in protest, "Who am I that I should go to Pharaoh and bring the Israelites out of Egypt?" (Exod 3:11).

For forty years Moses was a shepherd. Shepherding was just about the least desirable job in the ancient Middle East. Furthermore, they were not even his sheep; they were his father-in-law's (Exod 3:1)! When you're eighty years old, living in your father-in-law's basement and managing his pets, that's failure on multiple levels. It yields insecurity on steroids.

Yet God had an answer for Moses: "I will be with you" (Exod 3:12).

God didn't reinforce Moses's ego with positive thoughts about himself or tell Moses that he had simply underestimated his talents. He didn't say, "Moses, look in the mirror and repeat after me: 'My name is Moses. I am above fear and tough as nails. I can walk through a sea.' Now, Moses, close your eyes and visualize yourself walking up to Pharaoh. See yourself taking him down. You're good enough, smart enough, and doggonit, Moses, people like you."

None of that. God said simply, "I will be with you."

Confidence comes not from awareness of your competence but from the assurance of God's presence.

Even so, Moses felt like he had too many disabilities. He was "slow of speech and tongue" (Exod 4:10), which most likely means he had a speech impediment. Maybe he stammered. At the very least, it's safe to bet that he didn't have the cavernous, Val Kilmer/ Charlton Heston-like voice that commanded immediate respect. He probably sounded more like Pee-wee Herman than Christian

Bale. Whatever the case, he didn't think he had what it took to get the job done.

His personal insecurities were amplified by his past failures. He had already tried this once. Scholars say his question *Who am I?* in 3:11 echoes the question that the Israelites had thrown in his face the first time he tried to rescue them: *Who do you think you are?* (Exod 2:14). Their doubts and insults had taken root deep in his soul.

BLINDED TO GOD'S WORK IN HIS LIFE

Ironically, Moses's insecurities kept him from seeing how God actually had prepared him for this task. For forty years, he led sheep through the very wilderness where God planned to take the children of Israel. This meant he knew things like where the mountain passes and watering holes were. As a shepherd, he had learned to manage unruly herds. His time in Pharaoh's palace had taught him how governments work, how to write law codes, and how to conduct himself in Pharaoh's court. In one sense, literally no one on earth was better qualified for this job than Moses.

In many ways, this experience at the burning bush should have been Moses's "*Karate Kid* moment," where Moses saw that God had been preparing him his whole life for this very assignment. (If you don't remember the *Karate Kid* movie—well, first of all, shame on you. Short version: Daniel is a loser kid who gets beat up all the time. He approaches Mr. Miyagi, his apartment custodian, and asks him to teach him karate. In response, Mr. Miyagi makes him wax his cars, sand his floors, and paint his fences for months. After several months, Daniel is sick of it and wants to quit. But then Mr. Miyagi shows him that through these tedious tasks he has learned the basic motions that will make him a great fighter.) In the same way, in the tedium of the desert pasture, God had prepared Moses to lead a great people. God had been writing Moses's résumé for months.

But God didn't appeal to any of that in his commissioning of

Moses. He simply replied, "I AM." In other words, "Moses, it doesn't really matter who *you* are. It only matters who *I* am."

Moses stutters back in response, "*But* I am not . . . *eloquent* enough. *Smart* enough. *Successful* enough." And God responds, "I don't need you to be any of those things. I am all those things."

When you say to God, "I am not _____ enough," have you stopped to consider who you're talking to?

YOU ARE NOT . . . BUT I AM

God doesn't really want the guy who *expects* to be chosen. "Ahhh, God, . . . wise choice. Clearly you have an eye for talent." Nope. If you have a list of reasons why you think you are a good choice, then you're going to clog the pipe. You're not going to lean on God for his power, nor are you going to give him glory when you succeed. God prefers those who know they are weak. Those who have no choice but to lean on him.

Dr. Adrian Rogers, former president of the Southern Baptist Convention, once looked out at his congregation of more than seven thousand and asked, "How many of you in here graduated valedictorian or salutatorian? Please stand up!" A handful of people throughout the auditorium stood up, and everyone clapped. "Now, if you were an all-American athlete, please stand." He went on, "If you went to college on scholarship . . . if you were homecoming queen . . . if you graduated with honors . . . please stand." By the time Dr. Rogers had completed his list of accolades, nearly one third of his audience was standing.

To those standing, Dr. Rogers said, "Well, I have good news for you and bad. The good news—God can use you . . . also. The bad news is that you are not his first choice. Those who have less to boast about are his first choice."

God only fills empty hands. He wants vessels, not tools. Tools are well-designed instruments. Vessels are merely conduits. God chose Moses because Moses was in a place where he would have to depend on God. God didn't need Moses's ability; he wanted his *availability*.

That's why God allowed Moses to fail and wander in the wilderness for forty years. *Feeling inadequate is a prerequisite to being used by God.* For forty years, God had been teaching Moses, "You are not," so at the burning bush he'd be ready to lean on the I AM. At the burning bush, God said, "My 'I-am-ness' overcomes your 'not-ness.'"

So do you feel insecure? Ha! Scripture says you don't even know the half of it! You're so weak that you can't even guarantee you'll be alive tomorrow! You're so powerless that it is a sin even to give someone an absolute guarantee of what you'll do tomorrow. You are like a wisp of smoke—even the slightest shift in wind direction, and you're gone (Jas 1:10–11; 4:13–14). In the scope of the universe, you're so small and insignificant that you don't amount to a grain of sand on God's ocean floor.

(At this point, you may be thinking, "What kind of chapter is this? Thanks, J. D., for making me feel so small. How can I ever have a bold faith after a pep talk like this?")

As Louie Giglio says, the point is not to make you *feel* small; the point is for you to realize that you *are* small.[1] God wants us to see that we, indeed, *are not*, but it doesn't matter because the God who calls us is named I AM. And he is not small. He is larger, more capable, and more willing to help us than we've ever imagined. You're not God enough. But he is.

When you're weighed down by insecurity and doubt, don't drum up feelings of self-empowerment. Don't look inward to find your spark. Don't tell yourself that you're unique, a snowflake, a Skittle, a rare and unusual gift to the world. Look to the "I AM" and lay your insecurities down at his feet.

Louie Giglio says that for every doubtful "*But I am not . . .*" we could ever come up with, God answers with a thunderous, "I AM."[2]

"Who could possibly be smart enough to figure this all out?" *I am.*

"How am I supposed to know which way to go?" *I am.*

"I'm not very skilled." *I am.*

"I'm not sure who I can trust." *I am.*

"Nobody is listening to me." *I am.*

"Why can't we get pregnant?" *I am.*

"They stole my retirement savings from me." *I am.*

"Everybody thinks I can't do it." *I am.*

"What if I fail again?" *I am.*

"I can't hold on." *I am.*

"I need a fresh start." *I am.*

"I need a drink (or a fix or a hit)." *I am.*

"I feel so alone." *I am.*

It doesn't matter what your insecurity is. The I AM is all that you need.

In the Gospel of John, Jesus repeatedly takes the name I AM and addresses it to the areas of our greatest need. To those in darkness, Jesus says, *I am the light* (8:12). To those who thirst, *I am the living water* (4:14). To the lost, *I am the way* (14:6). To the confused, *I am the truth* (14:6). To those under the curse of death, *I am the life* (11:25). To those who feel insufficient, *I am the Good Shepherd* (10:14). To those who need a fresh start, *I am the door* (10:9).

God doesn't come looking for assistance; he comes as the great I AM. This means he's not limited by your inability. Neither your past failures nor your present struggles hinder him in the slightest. His call—to Moses and now to us—is to lay down our insufficiencies at the feet of his infinite strength.

To the unrighteous, he says, *I will be your righteous covering.* To the powerless, *I will be your defense.* To the empty, *I will be your fullness.* To the defeated, *I'll be your living hope.* To the dead, *I'll be your resurrection.* This is not a pep talk. It is the gospel.

Feel like you're not enough?

You aren't. But he is.

DO NOT TAKE THE NAME OF THE LORD YOUR GOD IN VAIN

When we question our ability to accomplish what God called us to do, we may feel like we are just being realistic about our limitations. In reality, we are insulting the God who called us.

In Sunday school I was taught that the third commandment, "You shall not take the name of the Lord your God in vain" (Exod 20:7 NKJV), meant that we shouldn't say "Oh my God" or "Jesus Christ" in frustration. (And in case Mr. Griffith reads this, I still agree that we shouldn't say that stuff.) But the command is about more than that. Specifically, we are commanded not to *take* God's name wrongly, which means attaching God's name to something without living up to the responsibilities and opportunities afforded by his name.

Think of it this way: There once was a girl named Veronica McPeters and on the greatest day of her life she became a "Greear." (Ha!) On the day that she *took* my name, everything that was mine instantly became hers. She had full access to my savings account and a claim on every day of my future. Failing to take that into account when she thought about her future would be taking my name in vain. Imagine that she had been poor and I extraordinarily wealthy, but after we were married she still refused to write checks from our account because she feared the balance was zero. She'd have taken my name in vain.[3]

You take God's name when you fail to live in the awareness of the strength God has placed in you. You may not realize it, but when you became a Christian, God's name, and all the assets that go with it, got attached to you. From that moment forward, you became his son or daughter, and you began to share in the life of the I AM. The apostle Peter says that we become participants in the divine nature and inheritors of all the divine promises (2 Pet 1:3–4; 2 Cor 1:20).

Don't miss the implications of this. When insecurity paralyzes us, and we think, "Well, I can't do this or that, even though God

212 ✝ NOT GOD ENOUGH

commanded me to do it," and we stop there, we are taking the Lord's name in vain. His name is now attached to us, and while we may not be _____ enough, God is the always sufficient I AM.

A friend of mine explains it this way: When you say, "But I am such a terrible mom," or "I am a failure," God replies, "I am neither of those things! And if I am in you, you are not either. What I am, you now share. Stop taking my name in vain."

You say, "But God, I am so dysfunctional." He says, "Yet I am so complete."

You say, "I am so deficient." He says, "I am so sufficient."

You say, "I am so doubtful." He says, "I am so faithful."

You say, "I am so sinful." He says, "I am so gracious."

You say, "I am so weak." He says, "I am so strong."

To whatever we are not, whatever we need, whatever we did not get from our parents or our teachers, whatever we are not getting from someone else, God thunders back, "I AM!"[4]

When the Pharaohs in our lives fling doubts at us, saying "Who do you think you are?" we reply, "I don't *think* I am anything. But I *know* the great I AM, and he is everything!" And when the haters in our heart whisper, "You are not," we shout back, "You're right. But he *is*, and I am in him."

So, name your insecurity. Call out where you feel weak, inadequate, or unable. Say, "I am not _____."

Go ahead. Right now, say it. If you can't say it out loud, find a piece of paper and write it down. I'll wait.

But don't stop there. Once you've named your insecurity, declare over it, "But in Christ, I am _____."

Sufficient.

Fully supplied.

More than a conqueror.

Righteous.

Pure.

Unstoppable.

God did not scan through the mass of humanity and pick you out because you were the most capable candidate. When he looked at us, he saw nothing but unworthiness. We were dead in our sins. We were people of unclean lips dwelling among a people of unclean lips. The gospel isn't that we were so awesome that he chose us; it's that *he* is so awesome that he saved us.

You become a Christian when you realize you're not righteous enough to save yourself. You start to be used by God when you realize you don't have the ability to succeed. God has to gift that to you as well.

In the Christian life, dependence, not self-sufficiency, is the objective. God wants people who are weak in themselves and strong in him. Don't let your inadequacies keep you from walking boldly in him. Instead, let these points of insecurity serve as invitations to lean more fully on him.

After all, if dependence is the objective, weakness becomes an advantage.[5]

Our weaknesses are places where we *naturally* lean into him. Our strengths are usually those places we forget him. Beware your *strengths*, not your weaknesses.

Confidence in the Christian life comes not from looking *within* at your talents but above to God's grace. If you are in Christ, you carry in yourself the *name* of the God who overcame sin and death. Your marriage, your finances, your future, your problems, unbelieving people—these are not overwhelming challenges for him. Embrace the great name of God bestowed upon you in Christ and never take that name in vain.

Then, begin to look at your world through the lens of what the I AM can do.

What kinds of things would you pursue if you knew the I AM was with you? That leads us to our final consideration.

CHAPTER 17

BOLD FAITH IN A BIG GOD

According to legend, one of Alexander the Great's generals approached him after many years of service and asked if Alexander would pay for his daughter's wedding. Considering the general's loyalty, it seemed a rather small request, so Alexander agreed. Alexander told the general to request the funds from his treasurer.

Alarmed, the treasurer returned to Alexander and told him that the general was requesting funds for the most extravagant wedding Greece had ever seen. Clearly, he said, the general was abusing his generosity.

Alexander thought for a moment, then said, "Give it to him. For my general pays me two honors. First, he believes that I am rich enough to afford his request, and second, that I am generous enough to grant it."

In the same way, the I AM is honored when we expect great things of him. As John Newton, writer of "Amazing Grace," reminds us,

> Thou art coming to a King,
> Large petitions with thee bring;
> For his grace and power are such,
> None can ever ask too much.[1]

God wants us to pray big things—things that reflect our belief in his awesome name. Scripture urges us to pray like Elijah, whose prayers altered the course of history (Jas 5:17). What do prayers inspired by the greatness of God sound like? In Scripture, they take on several important characteristics.

BOLD PRAYER JOINS GOD IN HIS WORK

Should we suppose that an awesome, omniscient God is primarily a cosmic genie ready to do our bidding? Bold prayer attempts to join God in his work more than it seeks to enlist God in ours. It begins with a humble posture before God, asking God what *he* wants. Jesus taught his disciples to open their prayers with "*Your* will be done, on earth as it is in heaven" (Matt 6:10).

I've heard it said that prayer works like a laser beam. Laser beams are created by stacking light waves on top of one another, channeling all the photons in the same direction. A handful of photons going in different directions yields only a soft, incandescent glow, but when you align the light waves, they yield a power that can cut through steel. In prayer, you stack the "wave" of your faith with the "wave" of Jesus's expressed promises, and that releases the laser beam of God's power into the world.

Scripture often tells us exactly what God wants on earth, which means when we pray Scripture, we pray with power. The Bible contains over three thousand promises, each one ready to be accessed by faith. To pray effectively, you have to know them. As I read through the Bible, I constantly look for divine promises to pray over my family, my church, and my community. I know lots of Christians who read through the whole Bible in a year. Why not also *pray* through it? Every time you see a promise in Scripture, ask God to fulfill that promise in your life. Sometimes you'll have to translate the promise into your context—God's promise to Abraham that he'd have a son when he was ninety-nine doesn't mean that you should look for a retirement home with a nursery—but ultimately all the promises of God are "yes" in Christ Jesus (2 Cor 1:20). Each promise points to something offered to us in Christ. In Christ, all the blessings that come with being a favored child of God are ours for the asking.

We know that God wants to glorify his name on earth through us, to supply our needs, to forgive our sins, and to deliver us from the destructive powers of evil at work in and around us. How do we know? These are the very things Jesus *told* us to ask for in the model prayer he taught his disciples (Matt 6:9–13). If we ask, he certainly will do them.

We know that God wants to use us to bring salvation to the world. In Psalm 2:8, he commands us to ask for it: "Ask me, and I will make the nations your inheritance." Global gospel advance is ours for the asking.

Here's a sobering question: How much is God *not* doing in the world—or in my life or yours—simply because we have not asked him to fulfill his promises?

To me, one of the saddest verses in the Bible is Matthew 13:58: "And he did not do many miracles there because of their lack of faith." "There" was Nazareth—Jesus's hometown! Surely, of all places, Jesus would have *wanted* to do miracles in Nazareth. He knew many who were suffering. But he did very little there—not because of his "sovereign will" but because of their unbelief.

I don't want to get to heaven and discover there were a lot of other things God would have done if I'd just asked. Written in my prayer journal are several things I've gleaned from Scripture that I believe God wants me to ask for. Not all of them are earth-shattering. Some are relatively small. Some of them are about my children. Others are about my church. A few are about entire nations. I have seen him answer some of these things already, and I am encouraged to pray for them all.

Sometimes when God answers one of those prayers, I feel like the little woodpecker that was tapping away at a telephone pole when lighting struck and split the pole in two. Dazed, the wood-pecker hovered for a moment staring at pole. Then he flies away, grabs a few friends, and brings them back to the pole, saying, "Yep, boys, there she is. Look what I did."

When I am doing what God asked me to do and asking for what he told me to ask for, I can expect the lightning bolt of his power. It's an incredibly exciting journey because when you know you are following the leadership of God in your life, you live with a great sense of anticipation. God may not always show up exactly the way I expect him to. But just like he showed up for Mary, Martha, and Lazarus, he'll show up for me at just the right time.

BOLD PRAYER EXPECTS UNLIKELY ANSWERS

My friend Vance Pitman leads a remarkable church right in the heart of "Sin City"—Las Vegas, Nevada. Vance is a gifted leader, but he will be the first to tell you that the success of Hope Church owes very little to his leadership gifts. The vision for Hope Church was not even born in his heart, he says. It began in the heart of a small, immigrant woman who moved to Las Vegas from the Philippines and started praying for a place she could bring her coworkers to hear the gospel. Vance explains:

> When God called my family to Las Vegas, you couldn't have picked a place that was farther off my radar. You see, I'm from Alabama. Where I grew up, people didn't go to Las Vegas. (Or if they did, they didn't tell anybody.) They don't believe Las Vegas is actually hell, but that you can smell it from there.
>
> But we knew God had called us to go. In our first week in Las Vegas, my wife and I were sitting at home when the phone rang. On the other end of the line was a Filipino woman named Lettie Peralta.
>
> She said, "Pastor! Can I tell you a story?"

I said, "Lettie, I don't know a soul in Las Vegas. You can tell me every story you've got."

Lettie replied, "Pastor, we've never met. I'm from the Philippines. I moved to Hong Kong to make money for my family. While living there, I met an American family and became their nanny. My family was very poor, so I sent most of my paycheck back to my family in the Philippines.

"That American family became like family to me. When they moved to the United States, I went with them. We moved to a suburb north of Atlanta called Woodstock. While living there, I heard a man named Johnny Hunt preach the gospel, something I had never heard before. It changed my life. But we weren't in Atlanta very long. Soon we moved to Las Vegas.

"That was a year and a half ago. Since we moved here to Las Vegas, I've been praying every day that Pastor Johnny's Church, First Baptist Church of Woodstock, would start a church in Las Vegas."

A few days earlier, my family and I had loaded up everything we owned in the parking lot of First Baptist Church in Woodstock, Georgia. Johnny Hunt prayed over us, and we got in our van and drove the two thousand miles to Las Vegas with *no idea* that Lettie Peralta was on this earth.

What I realized that day was that—contrary to what I'd thought—we didn't move to Las Vegas to start something. We went there to get in on something that God was doing long before we ever got there. We'd followed him there in obedience, and the urging to ask him to do something big in Las Vegas was an invitation from him to ask for something he already wanted to do.

We're now fourteen years into that journey. We've seen thousands of people come to Christ in our church. We've had the privilege of planting ten more churches in Las Vegas.

Sometimes people call and ask for our secret. "Pastor," they say, "How'd you do it? What was your strategy?"

Here's all I know to say: one lady from the Philippines grabbed ahold of the throne of God and she refused to let go until God moved. Lettie was desperate.

You dig deep enough into any move of God, anywhere in the world, at any point in history, and I'll tell you what you're going to find: men and women of God on their face, desperately seeking God. You'll never hear their names at a conference. They're not publishing any books. They're just hungry for God.

Do we realize the power that God has made available for the spread of the gospel? Do we realize how *willing* he is to move? Thou art coming to a King, so *large* petitions with thee bring, for his grace and power are such, none can ever ask too much!

God wouldn't have commanded us to ask if he didn't intend to answer. In what areas of your life are you not availing yourself of your divine opportunity?

BOLD PRAYER NEVER GIVES UP

It's easy to get depressed when we consider the bleakness of the world around us. However, I assure you that God isn't in heaven thinking, "Maybe I was too hasty with that 'every nation' promise. I failed to consider the power of the media! And the sexual revolution really set things back. Who could have seen ISIS coming? Plus, seriously—neither the Democrats nor Republicans can put forward a decent candidate for president? And that Kim Jong-Un is really proving to be one tough bird."

The king's heart, Proverbs tells us, is like a river in the hand of the Lord, and he turns it whatever way he chooses (21:1). The power of the nations is only a "drop in a bucket" (Isa 40:15). When we pray with an awareness of his awesome power, we pray with the earnest expectation that he can and will move things toward his appointed ends, even in the face of insurmountable obstacles. He delights in showing us how he accomplishes the impossible.

Many Christians make the mistake of thinking that God's mightiest works are things of the past. Evidently, that's what the people in the prophet Amos's day had begun to think too. God rebuked them: "This is what the LORD says to Israel: . . . 'Do not seek Bethel, do not go to Gilgal, do not journey to Beersheba. . . . Seek the LORD and live'" (Amos 5:4–6).

Now, that may sound like a random list of ancient Middle Eastern cities to us, but those cities didn't sound random to the Israelites in Amos's day. At *Bethel*, God renewed his promise to Jacob to make of him a great nation (Gen 35:9–15). At *Gilgal*, the children of Israel emerged from their forty-year wandering in the wilderness and renewed their covenant with God. There, God rolled away their reproach, parted the waters of the Jordan River, and knocked down the walls of Jericho (Josh 5:9). At *Beersheba*, God gave Abraham possession of the promised land (Gen 21:22–34).

Each of these places represented a time when heaven moved powerfully on earth.[2] The Israelites commemorated these places and spoke reverently of them. Evidently, however, they began to assume that these great outpourings of God's power were a thing of the past. They probably said things like: "Wouldn't it have been awesome to have been there when our father Jacob got his vision of heaven? Or to march with Joshua's armies and see God tear down the walls of Jericho?"

God said to them (and I'm loosely paraphrasing here): "Would you shut up about Bethel? I am sick of hearing about Beersheba! Seek me now—*in your generation*—and live. I am not the God of the past, I am the God of the present. My name is not *I was*, but I AM."

I wonder if, in our day, God might say to us, "I'm sick of hearing you always talk about the Great Awakening! I'm tired of hearing how awesome it would have been to have been a part of the early church. I'm weary of all your talk about the courage of Martin Luther and the success of Billy Graham. I want to move in *your* generation."

Monuments to God's past works should only serve as catalysts for faith in the present. When they don't, our admiration of God's past works wearies him! He is a God ready to act mightily for his people *today*.

Which direction do you look when you think about God's great outpourings of power? Toward the future or in the past? Pray as if you believe God's greatest works are ahead of you.

Based on what I read in the Bible, we have a lot of great stuff ahead of us. There are still more than six thousand unreached people groups in the world, and Jesus told us that before history ends, a thriving gospel witness will exist in each one (Matt 24:14; Rev 5:9). *So ask!* Somewhere, in one of our lives, is the next apostle Paul, who will bring an entire nation to Christ. Ask God to lead you to him or her! Or maybe it's you!

You probably have neighbors, friends, and family members who have yet to believe the gospel. That burden in your heart for them is proof that God is not done working on them. *So ask!*

This is not a time to hunker down and wait for the end. This is a day for bold, audacious, and hope-filled prayer to a glorious, awesome, and willing God.

BOLD PRAYER RESTS IN GOD'S SOVEREIGNTY

Every sincere Christian I know can recount times when they asked something of God they believed he wanted to give, but God didn't give it like they'd hoped. C. S. Lewis talked about praying to God during a particularly difficult season and feeling like he received "a door slammed in [my] face, and a sound of bolting and double bolting on the inside. After that, silence. You may as well turn away. The longer [I waited], the more emphatic the silence became."[3] (Somehow that quote never makes it onto anybody's Pinterest wall of "Favorite C. S. Lewis Quotes.")

The apostle Paul recounts pleading with God on three different occasions to remove a "thorn" from his flesh. All three times the only answer he got was "no" (2 Cor 12:7–9). Eventually, God told him to *stop* asking.

Bold prayer recognizes that we pray to a perfectly good, sovereign God. So when we pray, we submit our will to his. Jesus tells us that we should pray like children who trust their daddy.

He asks, "Which of you fathers, if your son asks for a fish, will give him a snake instead?" (Luke 11:11). Have you ever known a parent whose kid asked for a fruit snack and in response, the parent said, "Sure, close your eyes and hold out your hand," and then placed a living scorpion into the child's hand? Your kid asks for chicken nuggets and you say, "No, sorry . . . no chicken nuggets. But here's a live cobra!"

Jesus said that if we, being "evil" parents, would not do that with *our* children, will the greatest Father withhold from his children something that they need? Jesus won't give us a snake when we ask for fish.

Think about the reverse of Jesus's statement also, because it's equally true: Will he give us a snake if we ask for a snake?

Sometimes we ask for things we think are good that, from God's perspective, are not. My kids ask me for things all the time that, *in love*, I deny them. This week my six-year-old son asked for his own iPad. I know he thinks that would be *great* for him, but I care too much about him to just hand one over with all its potential dangers. He's also asked me if he can play with the hairdryer in the bathtub. I denied that request too, not in spite of my love for him but because of it.

Don't we think our perfectly good, infinitely wise heavenly Father will sometimes do the same with us?

Sometimes God answers our prayers by giving us what we would have asked for had we known what he knows.[4]

Bold prayers not only believe that, they rest in it.

BOLD PRAYER ACTIVATES GOD'S POWER

Finally, bold prayer unleashes a power that can only be accessed by audacious faith.

Throughout the Gospels, Jesus responds to bold faith—faith that at times seems even presumptuous. Perhaps this is best illustrated in Luke's account of the diseased woman who sneaks up behind Jesus and grabs ahold of his garment (Luke 8:43–48).

Hundreds of people mobbed Jesus that day, but when this woman clutched the hem of his garment, he turned around and said, "Who touched me?" His disciples ask him what he could possibly mean, since people were mobbing him from all directions. "No," he said, "someone touched me, for I perceive that power has gone out from me" (8:46 ESV).

What most intrigues me is that Jesus talks about his power as if he wasn't in control of it, like it's reflexive. He speaks of it passively: "I perceive that power has gone out from me." Aren't we talking about the sovereign God? Was Jesus not sovereign over the release his power?

Of course he was. But I believe the story is told this way to show us that Jesus's response to faith is so *reliable* that it might as well be an involuntary reflex.

When you reach out to Jesus in faith, he responds. It's as consistent and reliable as a reflex. The reverse is also true. Until we reach out in faith, he will not release his power. You can be around him, pressing in on him from every side, but until you reach out to him in faith like that woman, you won't experience his power.

Does that mess with your idea of God's sovereignty? Me too. I can't tell you how it all works together. But few things are clearer in Scripture than the reliability of Jesus's response to faith.

Faith activates a power from God, a power withheld *until* we believe. Think about Peter when he walked on water (Matt 14:22–33). *While* he believed, he stayed on top, but when he stopped believing, the power disappeared. Did that mean it was God's *sovereign* will for Peter to sink? I don't know. Maybe. But that seems like the wrong question to ask. The way Matthew tells the story leads us to assume that if Peter had continued to believe, he would have continued to stay on top of the waves.

This is not to say that we control God with our faith, but that in his sovereignty he has conditioned the outpouring of his power on the exercise of our faith. When we trust him, he moves; when we don't, he doesn't.

It's not long, drawn-out prayers that coerce Jesus to move. It's faith. In fact, Jesus criticized those who thought God would hear them for their "much speaking" (Matt 6:7 KJV). I make this distinction because I tend to pray about things at great length without ever trusting God with them, as if God will hear my "much speaking." So after I finish praying about something, I've started saying to God, "God, I now *trust* you with this." I want to remind myself that prayer is not primarily about *telling* God about my needs but *trusting* him with them. When I trust things to him, he moves.

For example, as a dad of four young children, I worry a lot about being the right kind of parent. What if I mess my kids up? Yet God promises that when I trust him with them, I can be confident he is faithfully at work even when I fail. When I entrust my kids to him, how they turn out is on him, not me. Does this mean my obedience is irrelevant? Of course not—it *assumes* my obedience. But it takes the pressure off me. I am leaning on his faithfulness, not my abilities, for their futures.

I think of it this way: If I found out that tomorrow I was going to die, I would be forced to trust God with my kids' futures. Would he be faithful with that trust? Of course he would. I'm confident his mercy would supply everything they lacked in my absence. *Can I not then trust in his faithfulness to them while I am alive?* If God's mercy could make up for my absence, surely it can also make up for my presence.

Recently our church staff took a short, spiritual retreat. One of the exercises we did was to rewrite Psalm 136 in our own words. In Psalm 136, the psalmist recounts several of the defining moments in Israel's history, and in between each phrase he pens the words "for his steadfast love endures forever" (ESV). The steadfast love of God had pervaded every stage of Israel's history. So I wrote out all major points of my personal history, and between each of the moments I wrote the words "for his steadfast love endures forever."

I then went back and read aloud what I had written, and as I did, I had a sudden sense of how faithfully God has worked in my life. He pursued me and shaped my life into what it has become. My parents were godly, but they did not engineer the most strategic moments in my life. God did.

Then I thought about my own kids. If God engineered the most strategic moments of my spiritual growth, could I not also trust him with theirs? I said aloud, "God, I trust you—not me—to accomplish your work in their lives." And suddenly I felt like, as a parent, I was walking on water.

This is leaning on a big and gracious God.

WAITING FOR THE WAVE

Several years ago, I stood on the shoreline of the Indian Ocean at the very spot where, just a few months before, a gigantic 70-foot tsunami crashed ashore, killing nearly 200,000 people. From where I stood, you could still see where the wave had stripped the mountains bare of trees. For miles behind me, houses had simply been washed away.

I lived and shared the gospel there for nearly two years. While there, I had prayed for God to send an outpouring of his power. I had labored for two years with almost no results. And now, instead of a wave of salvation, God sent a tsunami?

I felt myself getting angry. *Why, God? Why?* Why did you send a wave of destruction instead of a wave of salvation?

I don't know the answer, but in that moment God moved in my heart in a way that was as clear and powerful as I've ever experienced. It was as if he said, "I *will* send a wave of salvation. I have promised in Scripture that I will. For now, I want you to believe that I will do it. Your persistent faith will release the wave of my power."

In most areas of my life, that's where I stand. I don't know the ins and outs of why God does all that he does. I've had to learn to trust him. What I do know is that he is a God of infinite wisdom, infinite power, and infinite love, and that he is worthy of my trust. I know that those who trust in him will never be put to shame and that they will be the instruments of the outpouring of his awesome power on earth (Rom 10:11; Matt 21:22). The primary work we do for God, Jesus told us, is *believing* (John 6:29). Believing that he is who he said he is and that he will do all he said he will do. Trust in Jesus is the most powerful force on the planet.

Bold faith in a big God comes not from having all your questions answered. It comes from recognizing that a Voice has spoken. That Voice emanates from a being whose sheer power and size boggles the mind. Bold faith believes in a love as wide as the universe, a love demonstrated through Jesus's voluntary death for a rebellious race. Bold faith then watches in amazement as an all-wise, all-powerful, ever-faithful God does what he said he'd do.

I don't understand all the mysteries behind the glorious, wonderful, and sometimes bewildering ways of God. But I do know what he wants from me. He wants me to stand humbly before him in awestruck worship. He wants me to stand in front of mighty enemies, on the wrong side of incredible odds, before impossible problems, and believe that he will accomplish everything he said he would!

He wants me to have the faith that moves mountains and splits oceans. To faithfully tap away at the telephone pole and wait for the lightning strike of his power. And when that happens, I will back away, probably a little dazed, and say, "I knew it. *I knew it!* I knew he would do it. He said that he would. What an awesome God!"

NOTES

Chapter 1: I Can't Believe!

1. Brother Lawrence, *The Practice of the Presence of God: The Original 17th Century Letters and Conversations of Brother Lawrence (Nicholas Herman) 1605–1691* (Maitland, FL: Xulon, 2007), 34.
2. "If the Reality of God were small enough to be grasped, it would not be great enough to be adored; and so our holiest privilege would go." Evelyn Underhill, *Lent with Evelyn Underhill*, 2nd ed., ed. G. P. Mellick Belshaw (Harrisburg, PA: Morehouse, 1990), 24.
3. Tim Keller with Kathy Keller, *The Songs of Jesus: A Year of Daily Devotions in the Psalms* (New York: Viking, 2015), Ps 68, p. 151.
4. A. W. Tozer, *The Knowledge of the Holy* (New York: HarperCollins, 1978), 1.

Chapter 2: Your God Is Too Small

1. To be exact, 31.69 years.
2. Quoted by John Piper in *Think: The Life of the Mind and the Love of God* (Wheaton, IL: Crossway, 2010), 194.

Chapter 3: He Is Not Silent

1. *The God Who Is There* is the title of a classic book on knowing God by the great, knickers-wearing European apologist Francis Schaeffer.
2. "Sometimes I believe in God, sometimes I don't. I think it's 50–50 maybe. But ever since I've had cancer, I've been thinking about it more. And if I find myself believing a bit more . . . maybe it's because

I want to believe in an afterlife. That when you die, it doesn't just all disappear. The wisdom you've accumulated, somehow it lives on. But sometimes I think it's just like an on-off switch. Click and you're gone." Walter Isaacson, *Steve Jobs* (New York: Simon & Schuster, 2011), 571.

3. C. S. Lewis, *Mere Christianity* (New York: HarperOne, 2015), 137.

4. Cf. Tim Keller, *The Reason for God: Belief in an Age of Skepticism* (New York: Penguin, 2009), 133.

5. C. S. Lewis, *The Problem of Pain* (New York: MacMillan, 1973), 81.

6. Peter Kreeft, "Dynamite in Prayer," http://www.peterkreeft.com/topics/dynamite.htm.

Chapter 4: Incomprehensible Wisdom

1. I wrote this story from memory, so some of the details may not be exact. I deliberately changed a few to protect Justin's privacy, but the essence of the story is true.

2. Bart D. Ehrman, *God's Problem: How the Bible Fails to Answer Our Most Important Question—Why We Suffer* (New York: HarperOne, 2008), 153. Emphasis mine.

3. The exact wording here is my own, as the origin of the quote is unknown, though it is commonly attributed to Monsbaré. See Frank Turek, *Stealing from God* (Colorado Springs: NavPress, 2015), 139.

4. C. S. Lewis, "Answers to Questions on Christianity," in *God in the Dock: Essays on Theology and Ethics*, ed. Walter Hooper (Grand Rapids: Eerdmans, 1970), 52.

5. Louisa M. R. Stead and William J. Kilpatrick, "'Tis So Sweet to Trust in Jesus." Public Domain. CCLI Song 22609.

Chapter 5: Untouchable Holiness

1. Cf. Gen 14:10; 2 Kgs 25:15; Rev 4:8. Alec Motyer, *Isaiah by the Day: A New Devotional Translation* (Ross-shire, UK: Christian Focus, 2014), 41.

2. Ben M. Tappin and Ryan T. Mckay, "The Illusion of Moral Superiority," in *Social Psychology and Personality Science* (2016): 6, http://journals.sagepub.com/doi/pdf/10.1177/1948550616673878.

3. I owe this cataloguing of instances to David Platt, who listed these in a sermon on Isaiah 6 given at The Summit Church, January 31, 2016.
4. Gregory Koukl, *The Story of Reality: How the World Began, How It Ends, and Everything Important that Happens in Between* (Grand Rapids: Zondervan, 2017), 64.
5. I owe this insight to Tim Keller in a meditation on Isaiah 6 given at Redeemer Presbyterian Church in NYC.
6. Quoted in Jared Wilson, *Gospel Wakefulness* (Wheaton, IL: Crossway, 2011), 41.
7. See Motyer, *Isaiah By the Day*, 41.

Chapter 6: One Choice

1. I have adapted Plato's analogy significantly, but the core concept comes from his analogy of the cave as recounted in *The Republic*.
2. John 14:9; 13:3; 10:30.
3. See John 11:42; 10:30 (one with God); Mark 2:5 (forgiveness); Luke 14:26 (allegiance); Matt 28:17 (worship); John 20:28; Mark 4:41 (weather); John 8:58; 14:20 (eternal and ever-present); Matt 5:44 (Scripture).
4. Among others, N. T. Wright, *Resurrection and the Son of God* (Minneapolis: Fortress, 2003); Gary Habermas and Michael Licona, *The Case for the Resurrection of Jesus* (Grand Rapids: Kregel, 2004); William Lane Craig, *The Son Rises: Historical Evidence for the Resurrection of Jesus* (Eugene, OR: Wipf & Stock, 2000); J. Warner Wallace, *Alive: A Cold-Case Approach to the Resurrection* (Colorado Springs: David C. Cook, 2014); Lee Strobel, *The Case for Christ* (Grand Rapids: Zondervan, 1998).
5. Josh McDowell, *The New Evidence that Demands a Verdict* (Nashville: Thomas Nelson, 1999), 164–202.
6. Erwin Lutzer, *Seven Reasons Why You Can Trust the Bible* (Chicago: Moody, 2015), 102.
7. Emile Borel, *Probabilities and Life* (New York: Dover, 1962).
8. Jen Waters, "Leaving the Dark Side," Washington Times, December 6, 2005, http://www.washtimes.com/culture/20051205–110548–3523r.htm; David Gates, "The Gospel According to Anne," Newsweek,

October 6, 2005, http://www.msnbc.msn.com/id/9785289/site/
newsweek/.

9. Anne Rice, *Christ the Lord: Out of Egypt* (New York: Ballantine, 2008),
   312–19.

10. John Piper's *A Peculiar Glory: How the Christian Scriptures Reveal
    Their Complete Truthfulness* (Wheaton, IL: Crossway, 2016) is
    immensely helpful for going deeper on this point.

11. I owe this helpful phrase to Andy Stanley, given in a sermon on faith
    I heard many years ago.

Chapter 7: You Don't Get Your Own Personal Jesus

1. I first remember hearing this analogy from Josh McDowell in a
   lecture on the nature of absolute truth.

2. I owe this helpful little illustration to Tim Keller from a sermon
   I heard him give on the exclusivity of Jesus from Acts 4:1–21 at
   Redeemer Presbyterian Church.

3. Karl Barth, *The Epistle to the Romans*, trans. Edwyn C. Hoskyns, 6th
   ed. (London: Oxford University Press, 1980), 44.

4. Keller says, "If my heart doesn't learn to trust [God's] word when it
   tells me things I don't want to hear, then my heart won't accept it
   when it tells me things I desperately *do* want to hear—about your
   love and forgiveness." Timothy Keller with Kathy Keller, *The Songs of
   Jesus: A Year of Daily Reading in the Psalms* (New York: Viking, 2015),
   58.

Part 2: God Is Good

1. Charles Spurgeon, "Christ's Love to His Spouse," sermon 2488,
   delivered at the Metropolitan Tabernacle, Newington, London,
   September 5, 1886, accessed online at https://www.coursehero.com/
   file/16741381/2488-Christs-Love-to-His-Spousepdf/.

Chapter 8: The God We Crave

1. "He had been naked, you see, of pretense, but clothed with divine
   light." Augustine, *On Genesis: A Refutation of the Manichees*, trans.
   Edmund Hill (Hyde Park, NY: New City, 2002), 88.

2. Pascal, *Pensées*, trans. A. J. Krailsheimer (New York: Penguin, 1995), §148 (p. 45).

3. Quoted in Tim Keller, *The Freedom of Self-Forgetfulness* (Leyland, England: 10Publishing, 2012), 22.

4. Ernst Becker, *The Denial of Death* (New York: Free, 1997), 160–67.

5. I have edited his words for clarity. http://www.elle.com/culture/celebrities/a2465/drake-looks-for-love-608879/.

6. C. S. Lewis, *Mere Christianity* (New York: HarperOne, 2015), 136–37.

7. The ESV says "Sheol," the Hebrew word for grave or hell.

Chapter 9: The God We Hate

1. C. S. Lewis, *The Problem of Pain* (New York: HarperOne, 2015), 120.

2. Bertrand Russell, *Why I Am Not a Christian and Other Essays on Religion and Related Subjects* (New York: Touchstone, 1957), 18.

3. According to Volf's interview with *Christianity Today*, Volf was "born in Croatia, Miroslav Volf came of age in communist Yugoslavia, where he witnessed the ethnic tensions between the Croats and Serbs. After the fall of communism in 1991, those tensions escalated into a bloody war" ("To Embrace the Enemy," *Christianity Today* [online], September 1, 2001, http://www.christianitytoday.com/ct/2001/septemberweb-only/9-17-53.0.html). "My thesis that the practice of nonviolence requires a belief in divine vengeance will be unpopular with many Christians, especially theologians in the West. To the person who is inclined to dismiss it, I suggest imagining that you are delivering a lecture in a war zone (which is where a paper that underlies this chapter was originally delivered). Among your listeners are people whose cities and villages have been first plundered, then burned and leveled to the ground, whose daughters and sisters have been raped, whose fathers and brothers have had their throats slit. The topic of the lecture: a Christian attitude toward violence. The thesis: we should not retaliate since God is perfect non-coercive love. Soon you would discover that it takes the quiet of a suburban home for the birth of the thesis that human nonviolence corresponds to God's refusal to judge. In a scorched land, soaked in the blood of the innocent, it will invariably die. And as one watches it die, one will do well to reflect

about many other pleasant captivities of the liberal mind." Miroslav
Volf, *Exclusion and Embrace: A Theological Exploration of Identity,
Otherness, and Reconciliation* (Nashville: Abingdon, 1996), 304.

4. Heb 12:22; Rev 12:3–9.

5. Miller narrates his struggle through the voice of a character
named Quentin in his play *After the Fall*: "I see now, there was a
presumption. That one moved . . . on an upward path toward some
elevation where—God knows what—I would be justified, or even
condemned. A verdict anyway. I think now that my disaster really
began when I looked up one day—and the bench was empty. No
judge in sight. And all that remained was the endless argument
with oneself—this pointless litigation of existence before an empty
bench." Arthur Miller, "After the Fall," in *The Portable Arthur Miller*,
ed. Christopher Bigsby (New York: Penguin, 2003), 262.

6. Hebrew: *'erek 'appayim.*

7. A word Eskimos use to calm their children, made famous by Jack
Nicholson in the movie *Anger Management*.

8. I took insight into this point from a sermon by John Mark Comer,
which can now be found in Comer's *God Has a Name* (Grand Rapids:
Zondervan, 2017), esp. chs. 4–5.

9. United States v. George Wilson, 32 US 150, January 1833, http://
openjurist.org/32/us/150/united-states-v-george-wilson.

Chapter 10: Scandalous

1. Judah Smith, "God Loves the World: John 3:16; Romans 5:6," sermon,
The City Church, Seattle, 2013. See also Judah Smith, Life Is _____:
God's Illogical Love Will Change Your Existence (Nashville: Thomas
Nelson, 2015), 12–17.

2. Daniel David Luckenbill, *Ancient Records of Assyria and Babylonia*
(Chicago: University of Chicago Press, 1926), 1:213, 1:146, 2:127, 1:146,
2:319.

3. J. I. Packer, *Knowing God* (Downers Grove, IL: InterVarsity, 1993), 125.

4. Donald Grey Barnhouse, *Expositions of Bible Doctrines Taking
the Epistles to the Romans as a Point of Departure* (Grand Rapids:
Eerdmans, 1952–64), 1841.

5. John Mark Comer, "God has a Name, Part 3," sermon. See also Comer, *God Has a Name* (Grand Rapids: Zondervan, 2017).

6. See Keller's excellent book on this story, *The Prodigal God: Recovering the Heart of the Christian Faith* (New York: Penguin, 2011).

7. Charles Spurgeon, "Christ's Love to His Spouse," sermon 2488, delivered at the Metropolitan Tabernacle, Newington, London, September 5, 1886, accessed online at https://www.coursehero.com/file/16741381/2488-Christs-Love-to-His-Spousepdf/.

8. Martin Luther, *What Luther Says: An Anthology* (St. Louis: Concordia, 1986), 821.

Chapter 11: How to Confuse an Angel

1. William L. Lane, *Mark: New International Commentary on the New Testament* (Grand Rapids: Eerdmans, 1974), 516.

2. Isaac Watts, "When I Survey the Wondrous Cross," *The Psalms, Hymns, and Spiritual Songs, of the Rev. Isaac Watts, D. D.* by Samuel Worcester (Boston: Crocker & Brewster, 1859), 478.

3. I owe this analogy to D. Martyn Lloyd-Jones, though I can't remember from which sermon it came!

4. Isaac Watts, "When I Survey the Wondrous Cross," 478.

5. David Platt, *Follow Me: A Call to Die. A Call to Live.* (Carol Stream, IL: Tyndale, 2013), 38.

Chapter 12: Catching Fire

1. Paraphrase of Luther on Matthew 22:37–39, in Gerhard Forde *On Being a Theologian of the Cross: Reflections on Luther's Heidelberg Disputation, 1518* (Grand Rapids: Eerdmans, 1997), 29.

2. D. Martyn Lloyd-Jones, *Joy Unspeakable: Power and Renewal in the Holy Spirit* (Wheaton, IL: Shaw, 1984), 95–96.

3. I owe this turn of phrase to Tullian Tchvidjian, who said it at First Baptist Church of Jacksonville during their pastor's conference of 2009.

Part 3: Bold Faith in a Big God

1. C. S. Lewis, *Prince Caspian: The Return to Narnia* (New York: HarperCollins, 1994), 141.

Chapter 13: It's Not About You

1. Martin Luther is sometimes translated as calling Copernicus a "fool," but in the cited translation, Luther just calls him a "fellow." Either way, Luther wasn't a fan. Luther wrote, "This is what that fellow does who wishes to turn the whole of astronomy upside down. Even in these things that are thrown into disorder I believe the Holy Scriptures, for Joshua commanded the sun to stand still, and not the earth." Luther, *Table Talk*, in *Luther's Works*, vol. 54 (Minneapolis: Fortress, 1967), 358–59.

2. Jonathan Petersen, "The Story of Reality: An Interview with Gregory Koukl," BibleGateway Blog, March 1, 2017, https://www.biblegateway.com/blog/2017/03/the-story-of-reality-an-interview-with-gregory-koukl/.

3. John Piper, *Desiring God: Meditations of a Christian Hedonist* (Colorado Springs: Multnomah, 2011).

4. John Piper, "God Is Most Glorified in Us When We Are Most Satisfied in Him," sermon, October 13, 2012, http://www.desiringgod.org/messages/god-is-most-glorified-in-us-when-we-are-most-satisfied-in-him.

5. C. S. Lewis, *Reflections on the Psalms* (New York: Harvest, 1986), 132.

6. J. I. Packer, *God's Plans for You* (Wheaton, IL: Crossway, 2001), 29.

7. I owe this great little analogy to Andy Stanley from a sermon he preached on Philippians 2 called "Canvas, Part Two-Wonderful Cross" at Northpoint Church in Alpharetta, GA.

Chapter 14: He Wasn't Late After All

1. "Everything about her deliverance tells of God's love and power. And we know that if He could bring a tiny helpless infant, not three months old, through such dangers in perfect safety, He could no less surely have saved the lives of her precious parents, had that been in

His divine plan for them." Geraldine Taylor, *The Triumph of John and Betty Stam* (Lewisville, TX: School of Tomorrow, 1994), 116.

2. John Piper, "God Is Always Doing 10,000 Things in Your Life," desiringGod.org, January 1, 2013, http://www.desiringgod.org/articles/every-moment-in-2013-god-will-be-doing-10-000-things-in-your-life.

Chapter 15: Burning Hearts, Flaming Tongues

1. Spurgeon, first from "A Sermon and a Reminiscence," *The Sword and the Trowel* (March 1873); retrieved from http://www.romans45.org/spurgeon/s_and_t/srmn1873.htm. Second from "Earnestness: Its Marring and Maintenance" in *Encounters with Spurgeon*, ed. Helmut Thielicke, trans. John W. Doberstein (Cambridge: Clarke, 1978), 82. The story about Spurgeon's answer to the question of whether those who have never heard can be saved seems to lack a definitive source, though it is commonly repeated.

2. Lewis, *Reflections on the Psalms* (New York: Harvest, 1986), 90–98.

3. Lewis, *Reflections on the Psalms*, 95.

4. From "Jesus Paid It All" written by Jack Fascinato and Ernest J. Ford.

5. Edward Judson, *The Life of Adoniram Judson* (New York: Anson D. F. Randolph, 1883). See http://www.wholesomewords.org/missions/bjudson8.html.

Chapter 16: Heaven at Your Back

1. Louie Giglio, *I Am Not but I Know I Am: Welcome to the Story of God* (Colorado Springs: Multnomah, 2005), 51.

2. Giglio, *I Am Not but I Know I Am*, 143–47.

3. I owe this great illustration to Steven Furtick, "I Know I Am" on Exodus 3–4, sermon, Elevation Church, Charlotte, NC.

4. Adapted from Steven Furtick, "I Know I Am" on Exodus 3–4.

5. Craig Groeschel says something similar—with different terminology—in his sermon, "The Making of a Man of God," week 1 of the Elijah series. Available online at https://open.life.church/resources/1397-elijah.

Chapter 17: Bold Faith in a Big God

1. John Newton, "Come, My Soul, Thy Suit Prepare," *The Lutheran Hymnal* (St. Louis: Concordia, 1941), 459.
2. I owe this insight to Mark Batterson's *All In: You Are One Decision Away from a Totally Different Life* (Grand Rapids: Zondervan, 2013).
3. C. S. Lewis, *A Grief Observed* (San Francisco: HarperCollins, 1961), 17.
4. I first heard a similar phrase from a sermon Tim Keller preached on prayer.

Jesus Continued...

Why the Spirit Inside You is Better than Jesus Beside You

J. D. Greear

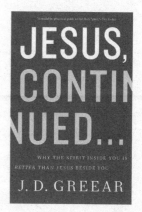

Jesus gave his disciples the audacious promise that the Spirit he would send to live inside them would be even better than his presence beside them. Yet how many of us consider our connection to the Holy Spirit so strong that we would call his presence in us better than Jesus himself walking by our side?

In *Jesus, Continued*... J. D. Greear explores—in clear and practical language—questions such as what does it mean to have a relationship with the Holy Spirit, how can we tell when the Spirit is speaking to us, and what do you do when God feels absent?

If you are longing to know God in a vibrant way, *Jesus, Continued*... has good news for you: that's exactly what God wants for you, too. His Spirit stands ready to guide you, empower you, and use you.

Tired of feeling burned out? Try being on fire.

Available in stores and online!

Gaining By Losing

Why the Future Belongs to Churches that Send

J. D. Greear

People are leaving the church J. D. Greear pastors. Big givers. Key volunteers. Some of his best leaders and friends. And that's exactly how he wants it to be.

When Jesus gave his disciples the Great Commission, he revealed that the key for reaching the world with the gospel is found in sending, not gathering. Though many churches focus time and energy on attracting people and counting numbers, the real mission of the church isn't how many people you can gather. It's about training up disciples and then sending them out. The true measure of success for a church should be its sending capacity, not its seating capacity.

But there is a cost to this. To see ministry multiply, we must release the seeds God has placed in our hands. And to do that, we must ask ourselves whether we are concerned more with building our kingdom or God's.

In *Gaining By Losing*, J. D. Greear unpacks ten plumb lines that you can use to reorient your church's priorities around God's mission to reach a lost world. The good news is that you don't need to choose between gathering or sending. Effective churches can, and must, do both.

Available in stores and online!